# REPEAT
# AFTER ME

## By Claudia Black, PhD, MSW

ISBN No.: 091022304-1

Published by
**MAC PUBLISHING**
**5005 E. 39th Ave.**
**Denver, Colorado 80207**
**(303) 331-0148**

1st Printing 1985
2nd Printing 1985
3rd Printing 1986
4th Printing 1986
5th Printing 1987

Other Works by Claudia Black

BOOKS:

**My Dad Loves Me, My Dad Has A Disease**
**It Will Never Happen To Me**

GAME:

**The Stamp Game, A Game Of Feelings**

FILM:

**Sound of Silence**

VIDEOS:

**Children of Denial**
**Roles**
**The Process of Recovery**
**Child's View**
**Criss Cross**

All of the above items available through
MAC PUBLISHING
5005 E. 39th Ave.
Denver, Colorado 80207
(303) 331-0148

# TABLE OF CONTENTS

**REPEAT AFTER ME**

# ACKNOWLEDGMENTS

During the time I contemplated and wrote *REPEAT AFTER ME,* I received a great deal of support that I would like to acknowledge.

Steve Wielachowski, Diane Murry, Diane Coll and Bill Reid were most helpful in the formulation of the exercises. I am appreciative of the feedback Patty Shryock, Mike Shryock, Diane Morshauser, Marci Taylor, Dave Landers, Victoria Danzig, Mary Carol Melton, Beth Reynolds, Wynn Bloch and Allan Campo offered. A special thanks to Allan for his musical notes that kept my spirits up when they faltered.

Marguerite Tavarez has worked diligently on the word processor in the creation of *REPEAT AFTER ME.* Thank you for your feedback, editing, patience and support.

Roz Schryver has been a delight to work with and I am grateful to her for her editing of *REPEAT AFTER ME.*

Becky Jackson, Tammy Carter and Debbi Mahon deserve a hearty thank you for their daily efforts in the production and distribution of all my work.

I have many friends whom are a significant part of my personal recovery process, but I would like to make a special tribute to Lorie Dwinell who was instrumental in helping me to begin the path that led to the freedom and choices I experience today. Also to my friend, Jael Greenleaf, who I thank for being an ongoing supporter and personal friend; and thanks to Lou Stoetzer whose acceptance and direction I value and trust.

Once again, I owe thanks to my husband, Jack Fahey. I thank you for your feedback, your re-writes, and your willingness not to tire with another one of my dreams.

The phrase adult child, while previously used in my writings to refer to adult age people once raised in homes affected by parental alcoholism is in REPEAT AFTER ME used to refer to any adult age person raised in a home in which that person as a child and/or teenager experienced many losses, whether as a result of an identifiable problem or a more nondescript syndrome.

For simplicity and clarity we have used the male form of pronoun when referring to a singular person.

*To the women in my family. To my grandmother, whose strength, energy and humor I admire. To my mother, who gave me love and the stability that allowed me to grow. And to my sister, Jana, whose childhood and adult childhood I've had the honor to share.*

# REPEAT AFTER ME

# INTRODUCTION

Once upon a time you were a child. That fact has an important bearing on your life today. As adults, we often try to ignore our lives as children and discount the impact it may have in our adult lives. *REPEAT AFTER ME* was written to be of help to you, the reader whose parents were not able to consistently attend to your needs, who were not able to help you believe that you were special and were not able to offer you a sense of emotional "safety" as you grew from childhood and adolescence into adulthood. These can be homes in which there is no identifiable problem ... homes where a family avoids showing feelings, homes where there is little nurturing, homes where rules are rigid rather than fair and flexible, and homes where time is not given to the children. When these dynamics occur in a family, it is likely you reach adulthood not feeling very good about yourself, having difficulty trusting people, having difficulty identifying needs and then allowing those needs to be met. These things can cause great difficulty in your ability to be close to others and create problems in your personal or professional life.

Should alcoholism, physical and/or sexual abuse or mental illness have been a part of your family, the consequences are even greater. It is very common that children of such families have difficulty asking for what they want, difficulty trusting, difficulty identifying or expressing feelings. It is common to have great fears of being rejected resulting in a tremendous need to seek approval. While an overdeveloped sense of responsibility is often characteristic, many of these children are not able to enjoy their accomplishments. There are often fears of "losing control" while they demonstrate an extreme need to control. Identifiable problems such as alcoholism, physical and sexual abuse often repeat themselves in the following generation. Whether or not there was an identifiable problem in the family, the child has experienced loss in his childhood. That loss is very painful and for the loss to no longer have side effects in the adulthood, it needs to be addressed.

While many people are able to reflect on their childhood and describe situations that were blatantly hurtful, other people experienced hurt by what did not occur — what wasn't said versus what was. To have a parent ignore you can be as hurtful as having a parent verbally ridicule you.

*REPEAT AFTER ME* is written to 1) help you recognize how your present life is influenced by your past, 2) allow you to release the parts of the past you'd like to put behind you, and 3) to enable you to take responsibility for how you live your life today. Freedom from the past means no longer having our lives dominated by our childhood years. It means no longer living in fear. In the process of freeing ourselves, we'll begin to say, "I'm angry that ...", "I needed ...", "No, ...", "It wasn't right ...", "I was only a kid ...", "Thank you ...", "I'm loveable ...", "It does matter ...". This can be said without blame and judgment.

*REPEAT AFTER ME* was not written so that you could blame your parents. I believe our parents did the best they knew how to do, yet, our parents' ability to raise us was often times limited because of some significant trauma in their lives. This trauma may have been physical, financial, or emotional. For most of us, our parents loved us. Yet many lacked the ability to consistently show that love. If they didn't love us, it was because they didn't know how to love — it was not because of us. They wanted it to be different but they did not have the ability to make it different, nor were they able to ask for help or accept help.

It is common for adults to feel guilty for wanting to reflect on how parenting during their childhood affects their adult life, often saying, "it wasn't that bad for me." No matter how severe another person's situation is, your own loss remains true. It is suggested that you do not compare your situation to another person's in order to ascertain whether or not you need to address these issues. What has occurred in your life is yours — your sadnesses, fears, broken promises, silent punishments, absent parents. Whatever your situation is, it's yours. It is not negated by anyone else's experience.

## LOSS OF RECALL

Some adults report not being able to remember portions of their childhood, as if they are amnesic. Most of us might expect that children from families where there was incest or battering might lose the ability to recall portions of their childhood. Yet, it is common that many adults who did not experience such blatant trauma experience the same lack of recall, sometimes for periods from months to years. There does not need to be a single traumatic event to cause lack of recall. Many people are raised in homes where the loss is emotional over an on-going period of time — or where trauma is of a chronic nature rather than an acute nature.

We must remember that we were only children; and at 5, 12 or 16 years of age we had the resources of just that — a youngster or an adolescent. Children, even older adolescents, have fewer psychological and physical resources than adults. Children from dysfunctional homes have even fewer resources than kids not raised in such homes. Children of dysfunctional homes become emotionally depressed, internalize guilt, repress feelings and become generally nontrusting. Socially, they become more isolated. They may have friends, but they aren't capable of honesty with these friends. At school, they may exhibit short attention spans and/or the inability to concentrate because they are preoccupied with thoughts of problems that face them at home.

These children may not have the physical reserves that other kids have, because they may not be getting the appropriate amount of sleep. Their sleep is often disturbed by nightmares. They may not be fed properly. Some children have physical problems related to stress — headaches, stomach aches, bedwetting (to a later age), asthma. In cases where children are physically or sexually abused, the physical trauma is even greater.

Spiritual resources for these children are often limited. While many children are simply never introduced to a religion or. faith, those who are familiar with religion often feel a great contradiction in their lives. "Is God truly a loving God"? "Why does God make people hurt like this"? These questions are normal for a child — yet the child is without the resources to seek the answers for these questions from a trusted adult. There are times in dysfunctional families where a parent may become fanatically religious, and the child's religious and spiritual involvement is motivated by fear or guilt.

Being a child of 4, 5, 10, 11 or even 14 and 15 from a dysfunctional home, you were a child with fewer resources than adults and a child with fewer resources than other children from unimpaired environments.

It is probable that if you have a major loss of recall, you had a need to defend yourself emotionally. Your thoughts and feelings were suppressed. You are not crazy. This phenomenon is very common.

Should you have a block of time from your childhood you don't remember, do the exercises in this book to the best of your ability. You will remember more of your childhood as you go through this book. Try not to become preoccupied with remembering what doesn't seem to be available. It is not necessary for you to have total recall.

## SHARING WITH FAMILY MEMBERS

After completing a few of the exercises in *REPEAT AFTER ME* the reader may be tempted to speak to family members about his/her past. This is not necessarily recommended.

Unless your parents have experienced a recovery process dealing with their own problems and/or if they feel good about themselves and no longer continue old behaviors, they will not understand what you are saying. They will repeat their old patterns of defense: ignore you, scream, blame, cry or give you token acknowledgment. Do not expect them to say, "I'm sorry", "I love you", "I was wrong".

If parents are recovered — their lives being very different today, they may be able to hear what you say. Yet be realistic, it will hurt. They won't like it. You cannot tell them how their parenting has affected you without their feeling pain — so if your goal is to tell them without hurting them — that is not realistic. Remember, it may be of greater help for you to share with them and allow them to feel their own pain than for you to remain quiet.

Sharing demands great honesty on your part. "What do I want to tell them? Why do I want them to hear that? Will it help me to say that to them? Am I saying this to hurt them?"

You may tell yourself you just need to say certain things out loud. If so, out loud to whom? Anyone? Or out loud to your parents?

If you choose to share your thoughts or feelings with them, it is best to keep your expectations low. The key to what you share with your parents should come from your own expectations. What do you want to happen or expect to happen when you share with them? Are you being realistic? Remember that in sharing, you can share what you want. It's not an all or nothing proposition. You choose the appropriate times.

Issues can be resolved without parental involvement. Most adult children will never experience their parents having a recovery process. The parents of many adult children have died. While it maybe impossible to resolve these issues directly with parents, it is possible to change behavior, say what needs to be said, hear what parents are unable to verbalize and come to a final acceptance of yourself.

Be cautious about sharing your new awareness  and self-discoveries with brothers and sisters as you are just beginning your own recovery process.  If you have been involved in a recovery process, (i.e. therapy, self-help groups) for a period of time, and you are feeling good about your own changes, you may share what you've discovered with siblings. But it is the tendency of adult children to give to others before themselves — or to give the awarenesses away before they have fully integrated new feelings and beliefs. As with parents, the key to what you tell your brothers and sisters is found in a realistic expectation of what will result from your sharing.

If you do share, remember that people experienced life within the same family very differently. Children are different personalities from birth, and each child enters the family at a different point in the family's evolutionary process. Many variables affect the development of different personalities in children, but one of the major considerations is that each child enters the family at a different place in the progression of various syndromes and illnesses that plague families. For instance, the alcoholic and co-alcoholic pass from not being alcoholic and co-alcoholic into early stage alcoholic — middle stage — to late stage. Those children who have access to either parent in the earlier stages or pre-stages have the opportunity for healthier parenting — and as a result, may receive more consistency and predictability. This leads to a greater sense of security, a more consistent show of love, assisting a child to feel a greater ability to trust. Typically the middle and younger children miss the opportunity to experience a healthy (even if sometimes short-lived) family environment. As a result each child has different perceptions and has learned a different style of survival.

For now, don't be overly concerned about what and when you share. Move through the book and become comfortable with your new awarenesses. In time you'll know what, if anything, you'd like to share with your family.

REPEAT AFTER ME was designed to help you take the steps of a process that will eventually lead to a greater sense of self awareness, self love and a more comfortable way of life.

As you complete these exercises, many of you will be experiencing new-found feelings and thoughts. This may be difficult — it will become more comfortable in time. Also, keep in mind that you don't have to make any big decisions regarding your past or your present as a result of your awarenesses or feelings. Just do the exercises. Receive the information.

It is suggested you have a support system that is aware of what you are working on. It will be important that you verbalize to others what you discover and how you feel. Consider who in your life would be supportive of your desire to grow. This may be a friend you write to or talk to frequently. This could be someone at work. This may be a family member. As much as we hope you'll receive support from family members, don't try to force the support from them. Your desire to reflect on your past is often something they don't understand. Choose to get that support where it is genuinely given. Many readers will find their greatest support in professional counseling. As well many readers can find support in self-help groups related to the dysfunction in their family, e.g. incest survivor groups, Al-Anon, Adult Children of Alcoholics self-help groups, Overeaters Anonymous.

These exercises are yours. Some of the exercises will produce great emotion; others will not. Some will quickly produce great insight; with others you may see the value only after a period of time. Please do them all. It is strongly suggested that they be completed in their specific written order. Do them slowly. Take them seriously. At times you'll complete questions fully, other times this will not be the case. There are no right or wrong answers. Nor will the completion of each question prompt a particular score of mental health. It is recommended that you respond in writing to the exercises. To merely think of your response is a way to stay intellectually defended. Have additional paper available as there may not be sufficient space provided for written response to the exercise questions. As you move through this book, remember that what you write is yours — your thoughts, your feelings. It is your perception, your reality. Try not to be judgmental of yourself. Know that you are not alone — this book was written because of the need of many people.

This book is not meant to be contemplated in its entirety in one sitting. The more you are able to be honest about your feelings, the better able you will be to assess your own speed. This process can be very impactful and it is suggested that after you begin the exercises you don't work any longer than one hour per sitting. It is also suggested you work on the exercises a minimum of one hour every week until you have completed the book. To move through the exercises too quickly may prevent you from feeling the impact of your awarenesses . . . yet to move too slowly may inhibit the momentum that is valuable in your recovery.

I found the following poem to be the essence of what I hope *REPEAT AFTER ME* offers you. May your journey offer the choices in your life you so deserve!

# AUTOBIOGRAPHY IN FIVE SHORT CHAPTERS

by Portia Nelson

## I

I walk, down the street.
 There is a deep hole in the sidewalk.
 I fall in
 I am lost . . . I am helpless
  It isn't my fault.
It takes forever to find a way out.

## II

I walk down the same street.
 There is a deep hole in the sidewalk.
 I pretend I don't see it.
 I fall in again.
I can't believe I am in the same place.
  but, it isn't my fault.
It still takes a long time to get out.

## III

I walk down the same street
 There is a deep hole in the sidewalk.
 I see it is there.
 I still fall in . . . it's a habit.
  my eyes are open.
  I know where I am.
 It is my fault.
 I get out immediately.

## IV

I walk down the same street.
 There is a deep hole in the sidewalk.
 I walk around it.

## V

I walk down another street.

# CHAPTER 1
# WARM-UP

**REPEAT AFTER ME**

## Family Tree
### EXERCISE 1

To better understand your family system, it is often helpful to have a mental picture of your family. Fill in the names of your family members.

**FAMILY TREE**

MOTHER'S SIDE                                          FATHER'S SIDE

Maternal Grandparents                              Paternal Grandparents
Grandmother/Grandfather                        Grandmother/Grandfather

_____     _____          _____     _____

Name Aunts with Spouses                          Name Aunts with Spouses

_____     _____          _____     _____

Name children                                    Name children

_____                                _____

_____                                _____

_____                                _____

_____                                _____

_____     _____          _____     _____

_____                                _____

_____                                _____

_____                                _____

_____                                _____

_____     _____          _____     _____

_____                                _____

_____                                _____

_____                                _____

_____                                _____

Name Uncles with Spouses                        Name Uncles with Spouses

_____     _____          _____     _____

**REPEAT AFTER ME**

Name children

_____
_____
_____
_____
_____
_____
_____
_____
_____
_____
_____
_____
_____
_____

Name children

_____
_____
_____
_____
_____
_____
_____
_____
_____
_____
_____
_____
_____
_____

_____

_____

**YOUR PARENTS**

| 2nd Husband (Step Father) | MOM | DAD | 2nd Wife (Step Mother) |
|---|---|---|---|
| _____ | _____ | _____ | _____ |
| _____ | | | _____ |

| Sisters & Brothers (Include Yourself) | Spouse | Children | |
|---|---|---|---|
| _____ | _____ | _____ | _____ |
| | | _____ | _____ |
| _____ | _____ | _____ | _____ |
| | | _____ | _____ |
| _____ | _____ | _____ | _____ |
| | | _____ | _____ |

_____  _____  _____  _____

                                                _____  _____

_____  _____  _____  _____

                                                _____  _____

_____  _____  _____  _____

                                                _____  _____

Indicate with a circle (O) the names of people whom you know who have experienced alcohol and other drug problems.

Check (✓) the names of people whom you know have experienced eating disorder problems.

Mark with an "X" the names of people whom you know who were physical abusers and/or were abused.

Indicate with a square symbol (□) the names of people whom you know who were incest abusers and/or incest victims.

Indicate with a star (★) the names of people whom you know who experienced other identifiable dysfunctions, and name the problem.

## My House
### EXERCISE 2

Draw a floor plan of the house in which you remember living as a child or teenager. (If you lived in more than one house, draw a picture of the one best remembered.)

Label all of the rooms.

Consider the following questions:

Which rooms were rooms that you liked? _____

_____

Which rooms were rooms that you didn't like? _____

_____

Where did you go when you wanted to be alone? _____

_____

Where did you go when you were angry? _____

_____

Where did you go when you were sad? _____

_____

Was being in your house different on weekends vs. weekdays? _____

If yes, how was it different? _____

_____

_____

With whom did you tend to spend the most time in your house? _____

_____

With whom did you tend to spend the least time in your house? _____

_____

**TALKING**

Most young children feel a great sense of loyalty towards their parents. Adult children often feel guilty when talking about their past and believe that they are being disloyal to their family. When you do the exercises in this book, you are not saying that your parents are bad people; you aren't saying that you don't love them. You are describing things that took place — attitudes, behaviors and feelings. What you write is your perception of what has occurred in your life. Your perceptions are your reality. There is great therapeutic value that comes by simply getting the past outside of yourself rather than keeping it inside. The energy it takes to keep the past within yourself can now be used for the present. There is a significant psychological relief in talking. When you talk openly, you are more apt to receive validation from others and not experience the ''alone-in-the-crowd'' syndrome. Talking honestly is the first step in creating a bond with others.

Most children raised in dysfunctional families found that it was safer (psychologically and sometimes even physically) to be quiet about what occurred at home. While most children developed a silent tolerance for the inconsistencies, untruths, sadnesses and angers, others spoke frequently about some incidents and problems with a sister, a brother, a parent. A few even spoke about their home life to people outside of the home, but usually on a limited basis.

## EXERCISE 3

Reflect on people you may have talked to about problems at home when you were a young child and teenager.

Check the frequency with which you can remember talking about problems to your:

|  | Never | Once | Occasionally | Often |
|---|---|---|---|---|
| Mother | ☐ | ☐ | ☐ | ☐ |
| Father | ☐ | ☐ | ☐ | ☐ |
| Brother (name) _____ | ☐ | ☐ | ☐ | ☐ |
| Brother (name) _____ | ☐ | ☐ | ☐ | ☐ |
| Sister (name) _____ | ☐ | ☐ | ☐ | ☐ |
| Sister (name) _____ | ☐ | ☐ | ☐ | ☐ |
| Other Family Member (name) _____ | ☐ | ☐ | ☐ | ☐ |
| Teacher (name) _____ | ☐ | ☐ | ☐ | ☐ |
| Counselor (name) _____ | ☐ | ☐ | ☐ | ☐ |
| Nurse (name) _____ | ☐ | ☐ | ☐ | ☐ |
| Clergy (name) _____ | ☐ | ☐ | ☐ | ☐ |
| Doctor (name) _____ | ☐ | ☐ | ☐ | ☐ |
| Friend (name) _____ | ☐ | ☐ | ☐ | ☐ |
| Friend (name) _____ | ☐ | ☐ | ☐ | ☐ |
| Neighbor (name) _____ | ☐ | ☐ | ☐ | ☐ |
| Neighbor (name) _____ | ☐ | ☐ | ☐ | ☐ |
| Other (name) _____ | ☐ | ☐ | ☐ | ☐ |
| Other (name) _____ | ☐ | ☐ | ☐ | ☐ |

## Not Talking
## EXERCISE 4

In some instances, certain issues were present in your family life as a child and a teenager that may have prevented you from talking about problematic areas of your life. Circle those that were true for you:

1. I felt ashamed.
2. I felt disloyal, as if I was betraying.
3. I was embarrassed.
4. I didn't understand what was occurring well enough to talk about it.
5. I was afraid I wouldn't be believed.
6. I was specifically instructed not to talk.
7. It was insinuated in non-verbal ways that I should not talk.
8. It seemed as though no one else was talking.
9. I believed something bad would happen if I talked.
10. I came to believe that nothing good would have come from talking.

If, as an adult, you still have difficulty talking about your childhood and adolescence, put a (✔) by the statement(s) that apply to you today.

If you do talk about your childhood, note to whom it is you do talk to.

_____

_____

_____

_____

_____

If, as an adult, should you still feel a sense of shame, try to understand that you weren't at fault — your parents would have liked it to have been different. Talk about your childhood — people will understand.

Should you still feel a sense of guilt when talking — trust that you are not betraying your parents, your family or yourself — if there is any betrayal, you are betraying the diseases or syndromes.

Should you still feel a sense of confusion about your childhood, that's probably an accurate description of how life has been for you — confusing. When attempting to explain irrational behavior in a rational manner, it will sound confusing. Talk — it will help things make more sense.

Should you still have difficulty understanding what has occurred in your family, read further and continue talking.

Should you still fear that you will not be believed, a great deal of information is available which will substantiate that these problems exist.

Should you have been instructed (specifically or non-verbally) not to talk, that instruction was motivated by fear. You don't have to live that way any longer.

The fact that you are reading this book indicates that you are aware that others are talking about their family problems. Talking is necessary for your survival.

Should you have experienced something negative from people you spoke with in the past — today, you are free to choose a healthier support system.

Should you have been conditioned to believe that "nothing good comes from talking", recognize today if you are still hesitant to talk, that you will only stay affected by the past. By talking, you will be able to experience the joy of the present.

# CHAPTER 2
# FEELINGS

**REPEAT AFTER ME**

As you use this book, you will experience many feelings which have been dormant for a long time. It is possible that you will be aware of feelings of loneliness, anger, sadness, fear and a general sense of vulnerability. Many times, as adult children begin to allow themselves to feel, they interpret that feeling as "feeling crazy" or "something is wrong". You are vulnerable and being vulnerable can be scary. It will be OK. Move through this book slowly and thoroughly.

Adult children often have difficulty identifying their feelings. While you may be aware of one or two of your feelings, you may not be able to identify other feelings. For example, you may be so consumed with your anger, you are unable to feel your sadness, disappointment or fears. Or, you may feel so guilty that you are unable to identify your anger.

As a young child, it is possible that you did not find it helpful to express your feelings — you might have been told that you weren't "supposed to feel that way," or "your feelings were wrong". Many times, your feelings were ignored. Probably the greatest reason one stops expressing feelings is that one perceives that nothing good comes from sharing the feelings. As an adult, not being able to express feelings contributes to feeling depressed, having difficulty in relationships and being unable to get your needs met.

Before we can better understand our feelings, it is important to talk about "control" and even more specifically "losing control". When adult children begin to experience feelings, they often fear losing control. This section will address what "loss of control" means for you.

The following exercises will help you to identify specific feelings and understand what these feelings represent.

## Losing Control
## EXERCISE 5

Create a comfortable setting, relax and close your eyes. Visualize what you fear might happen should you lose control.

Losing control means _____

_____

_____

_____

_____

_____

_____

_____

_____

_____

_____

_____

_____

_____

_____

_____

For most adult children, losing control means showing their feelings. Adult children who have repressed feelings often fear that when they cry, they will become hysterical or when they are angry, they will hurt someone else, or possibly hurt themselves in their rage. Control is often perceived as a black/white — all or nothing issue.

Examples of people's perceptions of losing control are:

"Losing contol means being angry, becoming violent, hostile or mean. I feel that I may physically hurt someone. I fear I will lose friendships and offend others."

"Losing control means starting to cry and not being able to stop."

"Losing control means letting out my rage until I start breaking furniture or hurting people."

"Losing control means saying something hurtful to someone."

Look at the statements you wrote regarding losing control. Whatever the fear is in losing control, usually the fear is far greater than the reality.*

Also remember, you are not being asked to give up all control, but to find flexibility where there has only been rigidity.

You may find it helpful to counter your fears about loss of control with messages that help you feel greater safety as you "give up control".

For example, you may want to counter your old messages with:

"Losing control *does not mean* becoming hostile; being angry can be okay."

"Losing control *does not mean* becoming hysterical; one can find relief in tears."

"Losing control *does not mean* 'bombing someone with nasty words', but letting them know what my needs are, which will be more helpful to me."

Other messages may be:

"I don't need to be in control at all times."

"I don't need to be in control if it means denying my wants, my feelings, my sense of spontaneity."

List two messages that you will find helpful to assist you in giving up some control.

1. _____

_____

2. _____

_____

*If you have been hospitalized for depression or have physically hurt someone else in anger and have fears that it will happen again, it will be important and helpful for you to share such thoughts about "losing control" with a trained, helping professional.*

## AWARENESS OF FEELINGS

Our negative feelings are more likely to lessen when we are able to talk about them. When we don't express them, they accumulate. Present-day disappointments, losses, angers and fears can become intertwined with the old disappointments, losses, angers and fears, making it difficult to separate old issues from new issues.

As you proceed to explore feelings, be aware that having a feeling does not mean you need to act on it. How one feels and what one does with those feelings are separate issues. For now, just be aware of the feeling. Try to view your feelings as a part of you — let the feelings be your friend, not something that will hurt you. Feelings hurt the most when they are denied, minimized or discounted. As you own your feelings and begin to feel them, be aware that you don't have to be preoccupied with all of your feelings all of the time. They aren't there to rule you, but to be cues and signals — there to tell you something.

Before you explore feelings, it will be important for you to know the value of being able to identify and express them.

Thoughts on this are:

— When I know what my feelings are and am more honest with myself, I then have the option of being more honest with others.

— When I am in touch with my feelings, I will be in a better position to be close to other people.

— When I know how I feel, I can begin to ask for what I need.

— When I am able to experience feelings, I feel more alive.

## EXERCISE 6

List four reasons it is of value for you to be able to identify and express feelings:

1. _____

   _____

2. _____

   _____

3. _____

   _____

4. _____

   _____

## Feelings
### EXERCISE 7

We have many feelings, some we are willing to expose to others, others which we choose to keep hidden. Identify the feelings you had in the age ranges below. Indicate the feelings you had shown as well as the ones not shown. The list of feelings is only a partial one; feel free to add your own.

Be aware that people often have more than one feeling at a time, and those feelings may seem contrary to each other. One can love and hate, be sad and angry, be fearful and happy at the same time. This does not mean you are crazy; it means you have reasons to be both fearful and happy, angry and sad or to hate and love.

**FEELINGS**

| love | anger | bravery | confusion | sensitivity |
| hurt | gloom | shyness | happiness | embarrassment |
| fear | guilt | patience | moodiness | understanding |
| hate | caring | jealousy | excitement | encouragement |
| worry | warmth | sympathy | frustration | discouragement |
| shame | sadness | | | |

| Ages | Expressed | Unexpressed |
| --- | --- | --- |
| Birth — 5 | _____ | _____ |
| | _____ | _____ |
| | _____ | _____ |
| 6 — 11 | _____ | _____ |
| | _____ | _____ |
| | _____ | _____ |
| 12 — 17 | _____ | _____ |
| | _____ | _____ |
| | _____ | _____ |
| 18 — 24 | _____ | _____ |
| | _____ | _____ |
| | _____ | _____ |
| 25 — 34 | _____ | _____ |
| | _____ | _____ |
| | _____ | _____ |

35 — 44  _____  _____

_____  _____

_____  _____

45 — 54  _____  _____

_____  _____

_____  _____

55 — 64  _____  _____

_____  _____

_____  _____

65 +  _____  _____

_____  _____

_____  _____

## SADNESS

There is always a great deal of loss in a home where you do not get the hugs you need, don't get the praise you deserve or don't get the consistent parenting that is provided in healthy families.

With loss there is sadness, and with sadness there is often tears. Feeling sad and crying are a natural part of being human. If you did not receive validation for your sadness — if you experienced negative responses when expressing sadness, you probably began to control the expression of such feelings.

Many adult children find themselves without the ability to cry. Others find that after years of seldom crying, they are frequently crying and are unable to identify the reasons why there seem to be an over-abundance of tears. The next few exercises are designed to enable you to identify your sadness and to help you to better understand how you perceive crying.

## Past Sadness

EXERCISE 8

Sadness in families is often caused by certain things that were said or that occurred. Yet, for many adult children, their sadness is caused by what wasn't said or what didn't occur. For some people, their sadness is for all of the times they had to move, from a parent never attending school events, or from never being told that they were loved.

Complete the following sentence:

When I was a child or teenager, I can remember feeling sad about (whether or not anyone else knew that you were unhappy):

1. _____
_____
_____

2. _____
_____
_____

3. _____
_____
_____

4. _____
_____
_____

Check the behaviors that describe what you did as a child when you felt sad:

☐ Cried when I was alone

☐ Cried in front of others

☐ Went to bed

☐ Took a walk

☐ Told someone about my sadness

☐ Other (fill in) _____

☐ Other (fill in) _____

## REPEAT AFTER ME

When I felt sad, my Mom usually: (Check the most appropriate answers)

_____ Never noticed

_____ Noticed, but ignored it

_____ Made me feel embarrassed or ashamed

_____ Made me feel better

_____ Other (fill in) _____

When I felt sad, my Dad usually: (Check the most appropriate answers)

_____ Never noticed

_____ Noticed, but ignored it

_____ Made me feel embarrassed or ashamed

_____ Made me feel better

_____ Other (fill in) _____

If there was a particular person — a brother, sister or other significant person in your life that responded to your sadness (either negatively or positively), describe how they responded:

_____

_____

_____

_____

_____

_____

_____

_____

## Crying
## EXERCISE 9

This exercise is designed for adult children who have difficulty expressing sadness with tears and for people who fear their tears. (See following exercise if you are a person who never cries.)

Complete the following sentences:

When I cry, I _____

_____ .

When I cry, I _____

_____ .

When I cry, I feel _____

_____ .

When I cry, I feel _____

_____ .

If other people saw me cry, I _____

_____ .

If other people saw me cry, they would _____

_____ .

## EXERCISE 10

If you were unable to complete the first lines of the previous exercise because you never cry, complete the following statements:

I never cry because _____

_____ .

I never cry because _____

_____ .

If I ever did cry, _____

_____ .

If I ever did cry, _____

_____ .

I might have felt better if I'd cried when _____

_____ .

I might have felt better if I'd cried when _____

_____ .

## Picture of Sadness

### EXERCISE 11

Draw a picture or do a collage of your sadness. Your sadnesses can be from your past and present experiences.

A collage is made by taking pictures, words and/or letters from words from magazines and making your own statement.

To make a collage, you need: 1) a 14" x 17" piece of paper, 2) Scotch tape, 3) a pair of scissors and 4) three to five magazines. Nearly any magazine can be used; it is suggested that there be an assortment. Allot 60-90 minutes to do your collage. (Complete it in one sitting.)

It is usually easier to begin your collage by flipping through a magazine and being open to what you see rather than looking for a specific word or picture. A part of the value in doing a collage is finding words or pictures that jump out at you that describe your feelings.

EXAMPLES: A Picture of . . .

1) a smiling person may represent what you did to mask your sadness as a child.
2) the word "blue" may describe a color tone to your sadness.
3) a cloud is meant to represent an intense amount of sadness and tears within you.
4) a woman may represent your mother, who reminds you of your greatest source of sadness.

Remember this is your collage. Only you will interpret the pictures or words. There is no right or wrong way to do this.

## Past Anger

### EXERCISE 12

Along with sadness, a great deal of anger is present when there has been a loss in your life. There are reasons for your anger — the many things that were said or that did happen as well as the words never said that you needed to hear, the times that were not spent with you and the lack of validation. Yet in learning to survive, much of that anger is never expressed — it is denied, minimized and discounted.

Complete the following sentence:

When I was a child or teenager, I can remember being angry about: (whether or not anyone else knew that you were angry)

1. _____

_____

_____

2. _____

_____

_____

3. _____

_____

_____

4. _____

_____

_____

If you have difficulty identifying your anger, you may want to think in terms of the words "frustrated", "disgusted", "irritated", "upset about". Sometimes changing the word will lessen the power of meaning and make it easier to accept. If that helps, go back to the previous exercise and try it again, only with your new words.

## Potential Anger

### EXERCISE 13

If you still have difficulty identifying your anger, try thinking of five things that took place in your childhood and adolescence that you could have been angry about. You may not have gotten angry or frustrated, but the situation was frustrating and the potential anger was there. Another way of looking at it is to imagine a young child — child at age 5, 7, 9, etc., and put him in your family in the same situation. Make a list of what this child could be angry about.

_____

_____

_____

_____

_____

_____

_____

_____

_____

_____

## REPEAT AFTER ME

Check the behaviors that describe what you did with your anger as a child.

☐ Pouted

☐ Screamed (at whom?) _____

☐ Was sarcastic

☐ Told the person with whom I was angry directly about my anger

☐ Hit harder on the ball field (or other sport)

☐ Ate to stuff my anger

☐ Ran away

☐ Other (fill in) _____

☐ Other (fill in) _____

When I was angry, my Mom usually: (Check the most appropriate answers)

_____ Never noticed

_____ Noticed, but ignored it

_____ Made me feel embarrassed or ashamed

_____ Made me feel better

_____ Other (fill in) _____

When I was angry, my Dad usually: (Check the most appropriate answers)

_____ Never noticed

_____ Noticed, but ignored it

_____ Made me feel embarrassed or ashamed

_____ Made me feel better

_____ Other (fill in) _____

## Expressing Anger
## EXERCISE 14

Adult children often have difficulty dealing with their anger. Many times they have no awareness of it. They may be frightened of their own anger, they may be frightened of other people's anger, or they may have so much anger they feel explosive.

If you have difficulty expressing anger, it is important to explore how you perceive your anger. Complete the following sentences:

When I am angry, I _____

_____ .

When I am angry, I _____

_____ .

When I am angry, I feel _____

_____ .

When I am angry, I feel _____

_____ .

If other people saw me angry, I'd _____

_____ .

If other people saw me angry, I'd feel _____

_____ .

When other people get angry, I _____

_____ .

If you were not able to complete the first five lines of the previous page because you are never angry, complete the following statements:

I'm never angry because _____

_____ .

I'm never angry because _____

_____ .

If I ever got angry, I'd _____

_____ .

If I ever got angry, I'd _____

_____ .

I might have felt better if I'd gotten angry when _____
_____ .

I might have felt better if I'd gotten angry when _____
_____ .

## A Picture of Anger
### EXERCISE 15

Draw a picture or do a collage of your anger. This anger is to be from your past and present experiences.

EXAMPLES: A picture of . . .

1) a volcano — may represent how explosive and frightening you perceive your anger.
2) a bottle of alcohol may represent that you often drink to get rid of your anger.
3) a dog, representing being mad at your dad for giving your dog away when you were a kid.
4) a car, typifying another form of escape when angry.

Refer to page 32 to refresh yourself on instructions for creating a collage.

People often have difficulty admitting and expressing anger because they believe getting angry means the cessation or withdrawal of love. Feeling angry doesn't have to mean a lessening of love. Being angry doesn't mean hating. Feeling angry means you feel angry — it does not need to have additional meaning. It is not a reflection of other feelings.

If you are a person who seems to have no difficulty identifying your anger because you are often or always angry, you may want to focus on your fears or sadnesses. You may not be aware of these feelings as they are probably masked by the anger. Often intense anger indicates that other feelings are hidden — covered by the anger.

If you are a person who has intense rage, you may never reach the point of not being angry, but you can get to the point where anger no longer interferes with your life. In particular, if you have been beaten or sexually abused and feel very angry, the intensity of your anger may lessen and you may no longer experience humiliation and sadness. But some anger will always remain. Again, the goal is not to eliminate a feeling, but it is to put that feeling in its proper perspective and to see to it that it doesn't interfere with your life.

### FEAR

Fear often plays a role in homes of affected families. While often experienced, fear is often denied. These fears, recognized or not, are carried into adulthood. In time, the adult child often becomes aware of a great deal of fear and is unable to identify it. This fear is often referred to as "unidentifiable" or "free-floating" fear. In some instances, this fear often becomes pervasive (ever present) or may appear episodically (appearing quickly and powerfully, then leaving almost as mysteriously).

## EXERCISE 16

Make a list of four situations that took place for you as a child or during your teenage years that you remember as being fearful whether or not you expressed that fear:

1. _____
_____
2. _____
_____
3. _____
_____
4. _____

Now, list the times you didn't allow yourself to feel fear, but the situations were fearful:

1. _____
_____
2. _____
_____
3. _____
_____
4. _____
_____

Check the behaviors that describe what you did when you felt afraid as a child.

☐ Acted like I was not afraid

☐ Cried

☐ Got angry

☐ Hid (Where? _____ )

☐ Told someone about my fear

☐ Other (fill in) _____

☐ Other (fill in) _____

**REPEAT AFTER ME**

When I was afraid, my Mom usually: (Check the most appropriate answers)

_____ Never noticed

_____ Noticed, but ignored it

_____ Made me feel embarrassed or ashamed

_____ Made me feel better

_____ Other (fill in) _____

When I was afraid, my Dad usually: (Check the most appropriate answers)

_____ Never noticed

_____ Noticed, but ignored it

_____ Made me feel embarrassed or ashamed

_____ Made me feel better

_____ Other (fill in) _____

## EXERCISE 17

To better understand how you experience fear as an adult, complete the following sentences:

When I am afraid, I _____

_____ .

When I am afraid, I _____

_____ .

When I am afraid, I _____

_____ .

If other people knew I was afraid, _____

_____ .

If other people knew I was afraid, _____

_____ .

## Picture of Fear

### EXERCISE 18

Draw a picture or do a collage of your fear. This fear is to be from your past and present experiences.

EXAMPLE: A picture of . . .
1) A person of the opposite sex may indicate to you that you are afraid of the opposite sex
2) The word "no" may represent how difficult you find it to say "no"
3) A hand may represent getting hit
4) A cartoon showing a person walking on a tightrope may represent how fearful life is for you

## GUILT

Guilt is a feeling children experience if they believe that they have done something wrong. Children often attempt to affect family problems — not recognizing that they are powerless to bring about the needed change. Because of their failure, they believe that they have done something wrong, and, therefore, they are guilty. There is a great deal of placing blame in dysfunctional families. Typically, when problems occur, family members blame each other — wives blame husbands, husbands blame wives, parents blame children, children blame parents, children blame each other. Young children, because they are defenseless, most readily accept and internalize the blame.

Adult children may not be aware that they internalized guilt as intensely as they have until they see themselves acting out the guilt by forever apologizing, taking care of others or having feelings of depression.

## Childhood Guilt

### EXERCISE 19

Check the boxes of the family members with whom you feel guilty for things that took place when you were a child:

☐ Mom

☐ Dad

☐ Sister (name) _____

☐ Sister (name) _____

☐ Sister (name) _____

☐ Brother (name) _____

☐ Brother (name) _____

☐ Brother (name) _____

☐ Other (name) _____

☐ Other (name) _____

## REPEAT AFTER ME

For each box checked, give two reasons which prompted your guilt. Example: "I felt responsible for Mom and Dad's arguing because they often argued about me.", "I felt responsible for my brother getting hit — I was older; I should have been able to stop my dad." or "I felt responsible for not being able to make my mom happier; I could have gotten better grades at school."

_____

_____

_____

_____

_____

_____

_____

_____

_____

_____

_____

_____

_____

_____

_____

_____

Check the behavior that describes what you did when you felt guilty as a child:

☐ Ate to stuff my feelings of guilt

☐ Hid (Where? _____ )

☐ Apologized

☐ Cleaned the house

☐ Tried to act "real good"

☐ Other (fill in) _____

☐ Other (fill in) _____

Check the most appropriate responses that describes what happened when you felt guilty:

When I felt guilty, my Mom usually:

_____ Never knew

_____ Reinforced my guilt by blaming me for things I did not do

_____ Made me feel even more guilty

_____ Punished me even if I was not at fault

_____ Made me feel that I was not responsible, therefore, helping to lessen my guilt

_____ Other (fill in) _____

When I felt guilty, my Dad usually:

_____ Never knew

_____ Reinforced my guilt by blaming me for things I did not do

_____ Made me feel even more guilty

_____ Punished me even if I was not at fault

_____ Made me feel that I was not responsible, therefore, helping to lessen my guilt

_____ Other (fill in) _____

## ACCEPTING POWERLESSNESS AS A CHILD

Because children have limited mental, physical and emotional resources, a major part of parenting involves physically and psychologically protecting the children — allowing them to be "safe". As children, we need security, love, happiness and honesty in order to grow and feel good about ourselves. Yet in many homes we find parents who are not able to provide these needs on a consistent basis. In dysfunctional families where parents are unable to supply the basic needs of the child, the child attempts to fill the void and assume parental responsibilities. But remember, these youngsters are young children — children who do not yet have the ability to act as responsible adults. Not only do parents often ask children to take responsibility for things for which adults should normally be responsible for, they often insinuate that their children are the cause of their (the adults') problems. Children oftentimes become confused. Children usually believe their parents "know everything" and accept their parents' every word.

As a result, young children have a distorted view of their power and often believe they can affect far more than they truly can.

**REPEAT AFTER ME**

## EXERCISE 20

It is important to gain a realistic perspective of situations that you have the power to affect. We all have power in our daily lives to affect many things — but being raised in a dysfunctional home, we commonly see power to be a black/white issue — we are either totally powerless or all powerful.

Reflect back on your childhood and adolescence and consider the things you feel guilty about and say "No!" to each situation. Then say "No!, I wasn't responsible for _____", or "No!, it wasn't my fault, my obligation."

Write "No!" in each blank beginning each statement and then continue by finishing the sentence.

1. _____ , I was not responsible for _____

_____

when  he/she _____

_____

2. _____ , I was not responsible for _____

_____

when  he/she _____

_____

3. _____ , It wasn't my fault when _____

_____

4. _____ , It wasn't my fault when _____

_____

5. _____ , It wasn't my duty or obligation to _____

_____

6. _____ , It wasn't my duty or obligation to _____

_____

7. _____ , I was only partially responsible for _____

_____

8. _____ , I was only partially responsible for _____

_____

Now write about anything else you might feel guilty about that wasn't your fault.

_____

_____

_____

_____

_____

_____

_____

_____

_____

_____

_____

_____

_____

_____

_____

_____

_____

_____

## Adult Guilt
EXERCISE 21

List names of significant people in your adult life. Then circle the names of those with whom you are feeling guilty:

1. _____    5. _____

2. _____    6. _____

3. _____    7. _____

4. _____    8. _____

For each person circled, give two reasons which prompted your guilt. For example, "I felt responsible when my husband wrecked the car because I should have gone with him and been the driver", "I feel guilty for leaving my wife", "I feel guilty for taking sick days from work when I'm not really sick."

_____

_____

_____

_____

_____

_____

_____

_____

_____

_____

_____

_____

_____

_____

_____

## Accepting Powerlessness As An Adult
EXERCISE 22

Believing that we only have the power to affect our own behavior, not the behavior of others, fill in the following sentences:

Today, I'm not responsible for _____

when he/she _____

Today, I'm not responsible for _____

when he/she _____

_____

It isn't my fault when _____

_____

It isn't my fault when _____

_____

It isn't my duty or obligation to _____

_____

It isn't my duty or obligation to _____

_____

I am only partially responsible for _____

_____

I am only partially responsible for _____

_____

Add some thoughts of your own about your sense of powerlessness today:

_____

_____

_____

_____

_____

## Identifying Feelings
## EXERCISE 23

People often live in fear of their feelings. Hopefully, now that you are in a more protective environment and are exploring what various feelings mean to you, you'll begin to view feelings as a part of you to be listened to and not to be feared. Allow feelings to be a part of you, an integral part that gives you clues and signals — a friendly part of you, not a foe.

The first step in allowing your feelings to work for you is to begin to identify the feelings you experience in the course of a day. At the end of your day (on the checklist below), check off the feelings you experienced. After a few days of doing this, you will find yourself much more adept at being able to identify specific feelings.

| FEELINGS | MON | TUE | WED | THU | FRI | SAT | SUN |
|---|---|---|---|---|---|---|---|
| angry | | | | | | | |
| sad | | | | | | | |
| guilty | | | | | | | |
| lonely | | | | | | | |
| embarrassed | | | | | | | |
| happy | | | | | | | |
| afraid | | | | | | | |
| anxious | | | | | | | |
| disappointed | | | | | | | |
| hate | | | | | | | |
| frustrated | | | | | | | |
| disgusted | | | | | | | |
| love | | | | | | | |
| lust | | | | | | | |
| compassionate | | | | | | | |
| confident | | | | | | | |
| jealous/envious | | | | | | | |
| affectionate | | | | | | | |
| excited | | | | | | | |
| bored | | | | | | | |
| confused | | | | | | | |

| FEELINGS | MON | TUE | WED | THU | FRI | SAT | SUN |
|---|---|---|---|---|---|---|---|
| numb | | | | | | | |
| hurt | | | | | | | |
| calm | | | | | | | |
| secure | | | | | | | |
| insecure | | | | | | | |
| silly | | | | | | | |
| playful | | | | | | | |
| shy | | | | | | | |
| remorseful | | | | | | | |
| ashamed | | | | | | | |
| nostalgic | | | | | | | |
| worried | | | | | | | |
| desperate | | | | | | | |
| resentful | | | | | | | |
| | | | | | | | |
| | | | | | | | |
| | | | | | | | |

After a few days of working the above exercise, you will begin to recognize the specific feelings as you experience them. This exercise is designed to work on the specific feelings that you are least able to identify. For instance, if you are working on identifying anger, stop yourself three times a day and ask, "Today, up until this moment, I was angry at _____

_____

_____ ."

If you are working on identifying fear, you would stop yourself three times a day and ask, "Today, up until this moment, I was afraid of, (or when, or that) _____

_____

_____ ".

After you've practiced this exercise to the extent that you are more easily identifying these feelings assign yourself the task of telling someone else about these feelings. Choose a friend with whom you feel comfortable sharing these innermost thoughts. Arrange to meet with this person on a regular basis. This could be a nightly telephone conversation, over lunch twice a week or other similar arrangements. The purpose of this is not for your friend to problem-solve with you, but for you to become more comfortable talking about your feelings.

Sometimes it is not in our best interest to express our feelings to the person toward whom we have feelings. An example would be a case with an employer who could be threatened and might retaliate. While our feelings in such cases are valid, we don't need to hide or swallow them; we simply need to rely on other outlets for relief.

When you know that you feel a particular feeling and choose not to verbalize that feeling, choose another manner that will help you to express it.

Outlets for feelings — positive feelings of joy or happiness as well as anger, sadness or fear might be to . . .

1) pound pillows
2) run
3) rip up newspapers
4) write
5) play and/or listen to music
6) meditate

Get the feeling outside of yourself. It becomes more tangible, less frightening — a friend, not an enemy.

Certainly the process of beginning to fully experience feelings is not always a smooth one. Some people go overboard in the discovery of their feelings and, for a while, talk about nothing else. Some people express their feelings in exaggerated form and are prone to be dramatic. As feelings become more natural to us, there is no longer the need for them to be "bigger than life".

While we do not act on every feeling, it is usually wise to consider our feelings when making decisions. Anxiety might tell us that we need to change something in our lives. Sadness might be a signal that we suffered some kind of loss and perhaps need to mourn. More favorable emotions like joy and excitement might spur us toward gaining more of the same.

The exercises 24 through 27 will assist you in identifying present feelings.

## Sadness Today

### EXERCISE 24

On the right hand side of the page list people that you have shared the specific sadness with or a person you are willing to share that sadness with now.

Today I feel sad about:

1. _____    _____ (name)

   _____

2. _____    _____ (name)

   _____

3. _____    _____ (name)

   _____

4. _____    _____ (name)

   _____

## Anger Today

### EXERCISE 25

List people that you have shared the specific anger with, or a person you are willing to share that anger with now.

Today I feel angry about:

1. _____    _____ (name)

   _____

2. _____    _____ (name)

   _____

3. _____    _____ (name)

   _____

4. _____    _____ (name)

   _____

## Fear Today
EXERCISE 26

List people that you have shared the specific fear with, or a person you are willing to share that fear with now.

Today I feel afraid about:

1. _____  _____ (name)
   _____

2. _____  _____ (name)
   _____

3. _____  _____ (name)
   _____

4. _____  _____ (name)
   _____

## Guilt Today
EXERCISE 27

List people that you have shared the specific guilt with, or a person you are willing to share that guilt with now.

Today I feel guilty about:

1. _____  _____ (name)
   _____

2. _____  _____ (name)
   _____

3. _____  _____ (name)
   _____

4. _____  _____ (name)
   _____

People who run away from their feelings suffer longer and often never recover from their grief. People who face their losses and all of the feelings that go with them become stronger and are able to begin to go on growing and living full and satisfying lives.

# CHAPTER 3
# SELF-ESTEEM

# REPEAT AFTER ME

## FAMILY DENIAL

The "acting-out" person in a dysfunctional family learns to discount or make light of their behavior. Other words for this process are to "minimize" or more strongly, "deny". Within the family of the alcoholic for instance, the alcoholic will rationalize his behavior — offer reasons that he believes justifies these actions. This "minimizing", "denying" or "rationalizing" is often verbalized to others. However, this is a process more for the purpose of the alcoholic convincing himself rather than convincing others that he is OK. The alcoholic, as with other acting-out people, finds this convincing necessary in order for him to continue his behavior.

While denial is necessary for the acting-out person, it often becomes an equally integral aspect in the lives of the rest of the family. Family members learn to minimize, discount or rationalize in their attempts to bring stability into their lives. In order to deny, people are required to be dishonest. Honesty will, for instance, sabotage the alcoholic's drinking and sabotage the family members' immediate attempts to bring consistency and predictability to a very chaotic, confusing family. Honesty, when applied in traumatic situations, will often cause discomfort and uproar. But the truth is that honesty will produce congruity and predictability on a long-term basis. Children learn to minimize, discount and rationalize for fear of the consequences should they speak the truth. Oftentimes when a child speaks the truth fully, he is told that what he sees is not accurate, "Your Mom's not drunk, your Mom's depressed"; "Your Dad's sick from the flu" (sick from drinking). "Your Dad didn't really hit you that hard. He's just under a lot of stress" (black eye, broken rib). This parental rationalizing and discounting serves as the perfect role model for the child to begin his own rationalizing, discounting and denial process.

## EXERCISE 28

In recognizing each family member's denial, it is possible to see how the whole family has been affected. Think about times your family discounted or minimized situations or feelings:

I can remember the time (Mom)  minimized  _____
discounted
rationalized

_____

_____

_____

I can remember the time (Mom)  minimized  _____
discounted
rationalized

_____

_____

_____

**REPEAT AFTER ME**

I can remember the time (Dad)    minimized
discounted  _____
rationalized

_____

_____

_____

I can remember the time (Dad)    minimized
discounted  _____
rationalized

_____

_____

_____

I can remember the time (Step-parent)  minimized
discounted  _____
rationalized

_____

_____

_____

I can remember the time (Step-parent)  minimized
discounted  _____
rationalized

_____

_____

_____

I can remember the time (Brother)  minimized
discounted  _____
rationalized

_____

_____

_____

I can remember the time (Brother)    minimized
discounted _____
rationalized

_____

_____

_____

I can remember the time (Sister)    minimized
discounted _____
rationalized

_____

_____

_____

I can remember the time (Sister)    minimized
discounted _____
rationalized

_____

_____

_____

## Denial

## EXERCISE 29

Reflect on your childhood and adolescence and complete the following sentence about five separate occasions:

I can remember the time I pretended (minimized or discounted) . . .

1. _____

_____

when in reality . . . _____

_____

2. _____

_____

when in reality . . . _____

_____

## REPEAT AFTER ME

3. _____

_____

when in reality . . . _____

_____

4. _____

_____

when in reality . . . _____

_____

I still tend to minimize as an adult . . .

1. _____

_____

when in reality . . . _____

_____

2. _____

_____

when in reality . . . _____

_____

3. _____

_____

when in reality . . . _____

_____

4. _____

_____

when in reality . . . _____

_____

As you work through these exercises, you'll begin to recognize situations where you minimize, deny and rationalize. Hopefully, this awareness will allow you to be more honest, to better identify your own feelings, and eventually to identify your needs. These skills lead to a likelihood of your needs being met and a greater ability for intimacy with others.

In addition, eliminating denial will also allow you to see things for what they are, which will alleviate long-range problems and allow you to begin to live in the "Here and Now".

## The Unspoken
### EXERCISE 30

While many feelings and situations were discounted, many things may simply not have been talked about or addressed at all in your family. Do a collage about the things people saw, heard or felt that no one ever mentioned or did anything about. When making your collage, don't be influenced by other people's sense of importance about these "unspoken" items. Ask yourself what you felt was important.

EXAMPLES: Picture of . . .

1) an automobile — may represent being with a parent when he/she was drinking and driving and never talking about it.
2) an attractive person — may represent your own attractiveness that was never acknowledged by your parent.
3) a Christmas tree — may remind you of a particular family fight that was never discussed again.
4) a trophy — may represent your being selected for a school honor; yet your parents didn't attend the awards ceremony.

When situations and feelings are not acknowledged, not only are they discounted, the person experiencing them feels devalued. This is very destructive to a person's self-image. Your willingness to acknowledge what has not been previously acknowledged is a step toward valuing yourself.

## FEMININE/MASCULINE

Children raised in dysfunctional families often have distorted views of masculinity and femininity. Because of these distorted views, adult children often assign a value or role to people because they are male or female, not because of their behavior.

Feeling good about masculine/feminine aspects of ourselves is an important element to liking ourselves.

## Being Feminine
### EXERCISE 31

Complete the following whether you are male or female:

Being a girl in my family meant _____

_____

_____

Being a girl in my family meant _____

_____

_____

Being a girl in my family meant _____

_____

_____

Being the (circle one) only, first, second, third, ( _____ ) girl in my family meant _____

_____

_____

## Being Masculine
## EXERCISE 32

Complete the following whether you are male or female:

Being a boy in my family meant _____

_____

_____

Being a boy in my family meant _____

_____

_____

Being a boy in my family meant _____

_____

_____

Being the (circle one) only, first, second, third, ( _____ ) boy in my family meant _____

_____

_____

## EXERCISE 33

My mom's femininity was something I (circle one)     liked     disliked

**What I liked**                                        **What I disliked**

_____          _____
_____          _____
_____          _____
_____          _____
_____          _____
_____          _____
_____          _____
_____          _____

Today, as an adult, being feminine means _____

_____
_____
_____
_____
_____
_____
_____
_____
_____
_____

## EXERCISE 34

My dad's masculinity was something I (circle one)        liked        disliked

**Liked**                                                **Disliked**

_____          _____

_____          _____

_____          _____

_____          _____

_____          _____

_____          _____

_____          _____

_____          _____

Today as an adult, being masculine means _____

_____

_____

_____

_____

_____

_____

_____

_____

_____

_____

_____

While there are stereotyped images of masculinity and femininity (e.g., "Men are big and strong, women are weak, frail"), hopefully the readers will find that feelings and abilities are not exclusive to any one sex.

People need to accept people for being people whether they are female or male.

## Self Esteem of Family
## EXERCISE 35

Many times, to the outsider looking in, what occurs inside a home is not as it appears. Families often portray a different reality to people outside of their family. Family members are often described as living behind masks. Circle the words that most describe how other people perceived your family when you were a child. Then circle the words which portray what it was really like from the inside.

| OTHER PEOPLE'S PERCEPTION | | HOW I SAW IT | |
|---|---|---|---|
| Happy | Caring | Happy | Caring |
| Loving | Quiet | Loving | Quiet |
| Warm | Loud | Warm | Loud |
| Safe | Scary | Safe | Scary |
| Insecure | Affectionate | Insecure | Affectionate |
| Angry | Violent | Angry | Violent |
| Hostile | Financially Secure | Hostile | Financially Secure |
| Distant | Financially Insecure | Distant | Financially Insecure |

## Self Images
## EXERCISE 36

When a child is raised in a family where everyone wears masks, that child usually grows into adulthood with his own mask.

Circle the words that you think would describe how other people perceive you now. Then circle the words you believe portray how you really are.

| OTHERS' PERCEPTIONS | | YOUR PERCEPTION | |
|---|---|---|---|
| Happy | Pretty | Happy | Pretty |
| Secure | Beautiful | Secure | Beautiful |
| Warm | Handsome | Warm | Handsome |
| Inadequate | Homely | Inadequate | Homely |
| Caring | Attractive | Caring | Attractive |
| Distant | Trim | Distant | Trim |
| Scared | Fat | Scared | Fat |
| Sad | Compassionate | Sad | Compassionate |
| Angry | Playful | Angry | Playful |
| Giving | Shy | Giving | Shy |
| Insecure | Confident | Insecure | Confident |
| Unhappy | Anxious | Unhappy | Anxious |
| Bright | Lonely | Bright | Lonely |
| Smart | Clumsy | Smart | Clumsy |
| Dumb | Graceful | Dumb | Graceful |
| Stupid | Talented | Stupid | Talented |
| Naive | | Naive | |

## Present Day Self Esteem

### EXERCISE 37

Adult children often have great difficulty feeling good about themselves. As children, they may have internalized a great deal of self doubt, powerlessness and shame. They lived in homes where they were not given consistent nurturing and validation. Positive stroking and attention was, many times, based on guilt, was inconsistent, intermittent or simply absent. While some children are more or less ignored in terms of their basic nurturing needs, others are frequently verbally discounted and berated.

Whatever the reason for not feeling good about yourself, it is now time to change that way of thinking.

You can often begin that process by allowing yourself to associate with supportive, nurturing people. A greater sense of self-esteem will emerge as you begin to believe in yourself.

Begin by focusing on yourself each day. Three times a day for two weeks, stop yourself (have the approximate times scheduled), and identify something you have done or said that was of value. The most minute and insignificant is acceptable as long as it is nice, considerate or of value to you. Keep a notebook to be able to reflect back. Continue this exercise until self-praise and feeling good about yourself have become automatic. Periodically repeat this assignment to keep these skills in practice.

For example: "I honked my horn in traffic" (vs. keeping my anger in).
"I didn't do a co-worker's work."
"I took time to exercise."
"I called a friend I hadn't talked to in a long time."

Prior to going to bed, either write on paper or speak to yourself in the mirror, thanking yourself for being you today.

Don't "Yes, but" yourself. Oftentimes in the beginning, you might want to discount yourself by saying, "I was honest, but not in every situation", "I said 'No', but I could have said it more today." You aren't striving for perfection. Don't focus on the parts of yourself that you don't like. Concentrate and acknowledge the parts of yourself that you do like.

## Accepting Compliments

### EXERCISE 38

In a healthy family, children are frequently given sincere compliments. Compliments are often non-existent, infrequent or insincere in dysfunctional families, e.g. "Dad told me how much he liked me, but two hours later he asked me to lie for him"; "While I received good grades at school, my parents never complimented me because they felt I should do well." In healthy families, compliments are accepted and believed. Children who didn't receive compliments or had difficulty trusting them have difficulty accepting compliments as an adult. Inability to accept compliments leads to low self-esteem.

Think about compliments that you received when you were younger.

What did people compliment you for? _____

_____

_____

_____

## REPEAT AFTER ME

Who complimented you? _____

_____

How did you feel, and what did you think when you were complimented? _____

_____

_____

_____

_____

_____

_____

Acknowledging characteristics that you like about yourself is a positive quality; this is neither wrong nor bad.

In unhealthy families, people don't like themselves. The acting-out person has a great deal of self-hatred. Spouses experience self-doubt and self-blame. Not being able to like themselves, parents find it difficult to teach their children how to feel comfortable with and how to validate themselves. Parents may ridicule you when they see you stand in front of the mirror. They may tease you about your walk, make derogatory comments such as, "So-and-so doesn't want to play with you because you're selfish, etc." All of these messages can be internalized to be accepted as "I'm not pretty", "I walk funny", "being selfish is bad", "other people don't like me".

Is it OK to feel good about yourself? If you cannot say "yes" quickly and believe it in your heart, you need to ascertain why you hesitate or say "no".

Sometimes we feel guilty when we feel good, when others close to us feel badly, e.g., "I don't have the right to feel good, because Mom feels so bad all the time".

Do you experience such guilt?

Old messages about not being able to compliment yourself need to be countered with:

"It's OK to like myself, to compliment myself."
"Liking myself does not hurt anyone else."

Add other messages that are relevant for you:

_____

_____

_____

_____

_____

_____

_____

_____

_____

_____

_____

When you have difficulty receiving or accepting compliments, here is a plan for becoming more open to yourself:

When you are complimented, pause for 10 seconds. After the pause, say "Thank you". (Do this out of courtesy if for no other reason). Then, pause again for another 10 seconds.

This pausing allows you time to accept compliments — it gives you less time to reject them or say "yes, but . . ."

At first, receiving praise may feel awkward, but with practice it becomes more and more pleasurable.

## CRITICISM

People who have difficulty accepting compliments are often much more open to accepting criticism. If you are as rigid in refusing to take criticism as you are in rejecting compliments you may have a running chance at feeling good about yourself.

As you listen to criticism, be aware that you only deserve to hear constructive criticism. When criticized, ask yourself if you think there is validity to the feedback. Would you like to see yourself be different? If you are able to hear and accept feedback but don't know how to behave differently, don't hesitate to ask the person offering criticism for thoughts on how you can do something differently. Constructive criticism is given out of care and if the person offering criticism cares, he will give more thought to your situation if you ask.

With criticism — hear it, evaluate its validity, assess how you would respond differently next time and move on.

Don't sit in it. Don't feel the total you is being criticized.

Being critical and judgmental is often a result of not liking yourself and not having your own needs met. It is important to take responsibility for your needs, and address the issues that allow you to feel better about yourself.

At the same time, try to be aware of your critical thoughts. When you find yourself aware of one, STOP. Pause for 10 seconds. Don't verbalize your judgment. If someone has done something that causes a particular negative feeling, you may certainly tell them about it, but rather than judge them as a whole person, take responsibility for your feeling. "I feel angry when you . . .", and be specific about this behavior. "I feel angry when you don't wait for me to finish my sentence." An individual is more likely to be open to your specific feedback as opposed to hearing a statement such as, "You're a stupid, inconsiderate person".

There is an adage about the glass being half full or half empty that is of value here. As you are able to work on learning what wasn't learned as a child, to now take responsibility for yourself, you'll find a greater sense of inner strength and love, and that glass will become half full rather than half empty.

## Stilted Successes
## EXERCISE 39

To feel good about yourself, you must be able to acknowledge and enjoy your accomplishments. Reflect on what the word "success" means for you.

Success is _____

_____

_____

_____

_____

_____

_____

_____

_____

_____

_____

_____

_____

_____

_____

Many adult children are not capable of recognizing or enjoying successes. For these children, a successful accomplishment must meet two criteria: 1) that it be nothing less than moving a mountain and 2) that it be acknowledged by all.

Success is not relative to others' accomplishments; it is a feeling of acceptance for an aspect of you.

Some adult children experience confusion in their identification with success — believing many times that they are a success in one endeavor, but a total failure in others.

If you identify with this, write a dialogue between one part of you that feels like a success and another part of you that tells you that you're a failure:

_____

_____

_____

_____

_____

_____

_____

_____

_____

_____

_____

_____

_____

_____

_____

_____

Read what you've just written. Does it sound familiar? Does it sound like someone from your past? Could it possibly be that you are parroting someone else's concept of success? Could it be someone from your family?

## EXERCISE 40

The following exercise will help you ascertain whether your concept of success is connected to your past:

As a child, in order to succeed at home, I _____

_____

_____

As a child, in order to succeed at home, I _____

_____

_____

When I did accomplish something, _____

_____

_____

When I did accomplish something, _____

_____

_____

## GREAT EXPECTATIONS

Many times in dysfunctional families, success (the accomplishment of a goal) is defined for children by their parents:

"You must graduate from high school"
"You must attend college"
"You must achieve good grades in school"
"You must get a good job"

Success for the adult child then becomes a "should". When a goal is realized (e.g., graduation), there seems to be no real elation — only a sense of "That's what I should do", accompanied by a sense of emptiness. College, good grades, a good job — even if these objectives are achieved, only fall into the "I should" category.

The unhealthiness of this logic is obvious. Children raised to think in the "I should" pattern can never truly enjoy success in their lives. Even when they win, they lose, because there is only the next goal to achieve. These children can never be happy with what they have or what they've accomplished. There are no successes obtainable for these adult children — there are only "I should's".

Are your accomplishments not enjoyed because they are simply never good enough? No matter how well perceived by others, you may discount the achievement because you think it could have been better. Many times, the phenomenon of, "it wasn't good enough" comes from our childhood behavior of misunderstanding the power we had. We often believed and hoped that if we were good enough or did something well enough, Mom might notice. Mom might tell me she loves me. Dad may take me somewhere. Dad may quit drinking. Mom and Dad may quit fighting. Mom and Dad might go back together. The truth is that no matter how perfect you would have been, your behavior wasn't the reason your Mom and Dad were as they were. Yet today, as an adult, while you do not operate from the attitude "If I do this, Mom and Dad will do that", the attitude, "It's still not good enough" has become a way of life.

Another major reason accomplishments are not enjoyed is the fact that before a project was complete, another project took its place. For children this happens as they manipulate their time in order to keep busy — to stay focused on tangible things in their lives — things that they could control. Not having a project may have meant having time to relax and relaxing meant "feeling", which was scary and threatening to survivorship. Not focusing on the tangible meant focusing on the intangible — the feelings, the drinking behavior, the depressed behavior — all things you couldn't control. So another project was necessary to allow yourself to feel good about yourself.

## EXERCISE 41

Make a list of childhood accomplishments experienced but not enjoyed:

1. _____

_____

_____

2. _____

_____

_____

3. _____

_____

_____

4. _____

_____

_____

5. _____

_____

_____

Now go back through your list, and note if the experience was not enjoyed because:

1. It was a "should".

2. It was never good enough.

3. I immediately got involved in another project.

## EXERCISE 42

As an adult, what accomplishments have not been enjoyed because they were:

A.   A "should":

1.   _____

_____

_____

2.   _____

_____

_____

B.   Never good enough:

1.   _____

_____

_____

2.   _____

_____

_____

C.   Moved to another project:

1.   _____

_____

_____

2.   _____

_____

_____

## Enjoying Successes
## EXERCISE 43

Learning to be able to enjoy your successes (small or large) means:

1. Pausing — taking the time to enjoy them.

2. Acknowledging that your behavior was of value. Understanding that it was of value irrespective of the influence it had on someone else or their reaction.

3. Allowing your behavior and your expectations to be based on what you genuinely want for yourself. This requires a lot of self honesty. It also requires the ability to think (and even to say "No!" to other people's "shoulds"). If you are imposing a lot of "shoulds" on yourself — stop to question them. Ask yourself "Why should I?" "Who says so?" "Do I want?" Try saying "No!" to a few "shoulds". See how it feels.

## ROLES

Children raised in dysfunctional homes typically play one or more roles within the family structure. These roles are identified as: The Responsible Child, The Placater, The Adjuster and The Acting Out Child. Adult children usually identify with at least two of these roles. Many identify with two or three at the same time in their lives; others identify with one role for a while and then clearly switch to a second role. With the adoption of each role, there are invariably negative consequences. Most people easily recognize the strengths of the first three roles, but fail to look at the deficits of each role. It will be important to identify your role adoption, the parts of that identity you'd like to keep and the parts you'd like to give up.

## The Responsible Child
## EXERCISE 44

The responsible child, otherwise known as the "9-year-old going on 35", has probably come to find himself as very organized and goal-oriented. The responsible child is adept at planning and manipulating others to get things accomplished, allowing him to be in a leadership position. He is often independent and self-reliant, capable of accomplishments and achievements. But because these accomplishments are made less out of choice and more out of a necessity to survive (at least survive emotionally), there is usually a price paid for this "early maturity".

For example: "As a result of being the "little adult" in my house, I didn't have time to play baseball, because I had to make dinner for my sisters."

Complete the following:

As a result of being the "little adult" in my house, I didn't have time to _____

_____

_____ because _____

_____ .

As a result of being the "little adult" in my house, I didn't have time to _____

_____

_____ because _____

_____ .

As a result of being the "little adult" in my house, I didn't have time to _____

_____

_____ because _____

_____ .

As a result of being the "little adult" in my house, I didn't have time to _____

_____

_____ because _____

_____ .

## The Placating Child
## EXERCISE 45

The "placater", otherwise known as the "household social worker" or "caretaker" was the child who was busy taking care of everyone else's emotional needs. This is the young girl that perceives her sister's embarrassment when Mom shows up at a school Open House drunk and will do whatever is necessary to take the embarrassment away. This may be a brother assisting his brother in not feeling the disappointment in Dad's not showing up at a ball game. This is the child who intervenes and assures that the kids are not too frightened after there has been a screaming scene. This is a warm, sensitive, listening, caring person who shows a tremendous capacity to help others feel better. For the placater, survival was taking away the fears, sadnesses and the guilt of others. Survival was giving one's time, energy and empathy.

But as adults, people who have spent years taking care of others begin to "pay a price" for the "imbalance of focus". It is most likely that there were things that were not learned.

Example: "As a result of being the 'household social worker', I didn't have time to tell anyone my problems, because I was too busy assisting in solving other people's problems."

Complete the following:

As a result of being the "household social worker", I didn't have time to _____

_____

_____ because _____

_____ .

As a result of being the "household social worker", I didn't have time to _____

_____

_____ because _____

_____ .

As a result of being the "household social worker", I didn't have time to _____

_____

_____ because _____

_____ .

As a result of being the "household social worker", I didn't have time to _____

_____

_____ because _____

_____ .

## The Adjusting Child
## EXERCISE 46

The "adjusting child" found it easier to not question, think about nor respond in any way to what was occurring in his or her life. Adjusters do not attempt to change, prevent or alleviate any situations. They simply "adjust", do what they are told — detach themselves emotionally, physically and socially as much as is possible.

While it is easier to survive the frequent confusion and hurt of a dysfunctional home through adjusting, there are many negative consequences for the adjusters in adult life.

Example : "As a result of adjusting/detaching I got into a lot of strange situations because I didn't stop to think."

Complete the following:

As a result of adjusting/detaching I _____

_____

because _____ .

As a result of adjusting/detaching I _____

_____

because _____ .

As a result of adjusting/detaching I _____

_____

because _____ .

As a result of adjusting/detaching I _____

_____

because _____ .

## The "Acting Out" Child
## EXERCISE 47

Some kids in unhealthy homes became very angry at a very young age. They were confused and scared, and they acted out their confusion in ways that got them a lot of negative attention. It was common that they got into trouble at home, school and often on the streets. These are kids who are screaming "There's something wrong here!" These are kids who don't find survivorship in the other three roles.

Example: "because of acting out behavior, I didn't have time to pay attention at school."

If this was true for you, answer the following:

Because of "acting out" behavior, I didn't have time to _____

_____

_____ .

Because of "acting out" behavior, I didn't have time to _____

_____

_____ .

Because of "acting out" behavior, I didn't have time to _____

_____

_____ .

Because of "acting out" behavior, I didn't have time to _____

_____

_____ .

## Adult Roles
## EXERCISE 48

Today as an adult I am still (check the appropriate boxes):

☐  Overly responsible

☐  Placating

☐  Acting out negatively

☐  Adjusting

## REPEAT AFTER ME

As a result, I still haven't learned _____

_____

_____

_____

_____

_____

_____

_____

_____

_____

It is important for me to take the time to (be specific) _____

_____

_____

_____

_____

_____

_____

_____

_____

_____

_____

Remember, with roles, you don't have to give up the good things you learned. Balance is the goal. As a responsible child, you won't have to give up your ability to lead and take charge, but you can allow others the opportunity so you have a break. As a placater, you may retain your sensitivity of these feelings but no longer at your expense. As an adjuster who is super flexible, you can trust your own ability to make decisions and not always be the responder. As an acting out child, you don't have to give up your anger, but you can find yourself asking for what you want in a more calm, direct manner.

# CHAPTER 4
# FAMILY ISSUES

**REPEAT AFTER ME**

## NEEDING PEOPLE

Many times, adults are not available when children need them. A child may need a kind word, a hug, help in solving a problem or validation. These things didn't happen as much as they needed to in problematic families. A kind word, a hug, help with solving a problem could have occurred ...

... when you had trouble at school
... when a kid picked on you
... when you were sick
... when you brought home an 'A'
... when you did well in sports
... when a parent hit you
... when you began to mature sexually
... when you started dating

## EXERCISE 49

Think about situations that occurred in which you wanted a parent or another important person in your life to respond and to make themselves available to you, and they did not.

Note the person (brother, sister, friend, teacher, lover, spouse) and the occasion:

Ages:

Birth-5   1. _____

            _____

         2. _____

            _____

6-11   1. _____

            _____

         2. _____

            _____

12-17   1. _____

            _____

         2. _____

            _____

**REPEAT AFTER ME**

18-24    1.  _____

_____

            2.  _____

_____

25-34    1.  _____

_____

            2.  _____

_____

35-44    1.  _____

_____

            2.  _____

_____

45-54    1.  _____

_____

            2.  _____

_____

55-64    1.  _____

_____

            2.  _____

_____

65 +     1.  _____

_____

            2.  _____

_____

## Finding People

## EXERCISE 50

As a child and in your adulthood, there were times when people were available. It's important to be able to acknowledge that fact.

List those situations in which a parent or other significant person did respond and did make themselves available.

Ages:

Birth-5    1. _____

_____

2. _____

_____

6-11    1. _____

_____

2. _____

_____

12-17    1. _____

_____

2. _____

_____

18-24    1. _____

_____

2. _____

_____

25-34    1. _____

_____

2. _____

_____

35-44    1. _____

_____

2. _____

_____

45-54    1. _____

_____

2. _____

_____

55-64     1. _____

_____

2. _____

_____

65 +      1. _____

_____

2. _____

_____

Put a star ( ★ ) by the names of people already mentioned who you could trust to be available to you today.

## Asking People for What I Need
## EXERCISE 51

The following exercise is to assist you in being able to identify your needs. Write a letter to each of your parents. These letters are for your understanding, not theirs. They are not meant to be delivered to either parent. Spend approximately 20-30 minutes on each, and write no more than three pages per letter. Allow yourself at least one week between the writing of each letter.

The purpose for doing these letters is:

1) It is often cathartic and moves you one more step through the grief process,
2) For many who do it, they recognize that there were things to be grateful for,
3) It aids in recognizing your childhood needs,
4) As a result of recognizing childhood needs, it is often easier to identify adult needs, making it more likely that you can now go about getting those needs met.

Begin by writing:

"Dear Mom (or Dad),"

Thank your parent for what he or she gave you, e.g., "I want to thank you Mom for always remembering my birthdays and making them special." "Thank you for encouraging me to play the piano. I still play. Thanks for coming to my school play in the 2nd grade. Thanks for letting me go to my girlfriend's house on nights when Dad was real bad."

Obviously, you could be saying in your letter, "Hey, Mom, where were you during my other school plays?" "Why didn't you leave Dad?" "Why didn't you ever play with me?" But pass on that now, and sincerely thank your parents for a few things that they did give you.

Then (after no more than six or seven "thank you's"), tell this parent what it is you needed from him/her that you didn't get. "I needed you to protect me from Dad. I needed you to tell me it was OK for me to be angry. I needed you to come into the bedroom and notice when I was crying. You never came in. I needed you to follow through on your promises." This is a much lengthier part of the letter.

If you have difficulty saying "thank you", you may want to do the second part of the letter first. Undoubtedly, for some people, what they have to be thankful for seems very small. That's OK.

Sign your letter when you have finished it.

After your letter is completed circle your needs and then ask yourself if those needs are still needs today.

Needs such as "I needed to play", "I needed to be able to make mistakes and not feel I was a bad person" are needs that typically are carried to adulthood. While those needs are not going to be met by a parent — they are needs you will have to take responsibility for meeting today.

## Saying "No"
### EXERCISE 52

Many adult children have difficulty saying "no". Yet, without the ability to say "no", you will not be able to establish appropriate limits or boundaries. The inability to say "no" results in being overextended, feeling victimized and used. More importantly, saying "no" is a vital part of assuring that your needs are met. If you cannot say "no", you'll never know if you're saying "yes" freely.

Complete the following about what happens when you say "no":

Examples may be "When I say 'no', I am afraid that people won't like me."; "When I say 'no', I sound like my mother."

When I say "no", I _____

_____

_____

When I say "no", I _____

_____

_____

When I say "no", I _____

_____

_____

## "No's"
### EXERCISE 53

Think about "no's" you've heard in your young life, e.g., you got a "no" when your application to a particular school was turned down, a "no" from prospective dates, a "no" when you tried out for a team but didn't make it.

List five examples of "no's" from your childhood and adolescence that were appropriate:

1. _____

_____

2. _____

_____

**REPEAT AFTER ME**

3. _____

_____

4. _____

_____

5. _____

_____

Now list five examples of "no's" from your childhood and adolescence that were inappropriate:

1. _____

_____

2. _____

_____

3. _____

_____

4. _____

_____

5. _____

_____

Have "no's" in your life made you angry? Explain: _____

_____

_____

_____

_____

_____

_____

_____

_____

_____

Have "no's" turned out to be helpful to you? Explain: _____

_____

_____

_____

_____

_____

_____

_____

_____

How did your mom say, "no"? Did she scream, "No! You can't". Or did she say "yes" and then sabotage the situation so it became a "no"? Did she ever say "no"? Was she fair?

Write about hearing "no" from your mom.

_____

_____

_____

_____

_____

_____

_____

_____

_____

_____

_____

## REPEAT AFTER ME

How did your dad say "no"? Was he ever available to say "no"? Did he say "no" before he heard the request? Was he fair?

Write about hearing "no" from your dad.

_____

_____

_____

_____

_____

_____

_____

_____

_____

As an adult, what do you hear when people say "no" to you? How do you feel? Explain.

_____

_____

_____

_____

_____

_____

_____

_____

_____

_____

_____

_____

_____

_____

_____

## Saying "Yes"
### EXERCISE 54

For people who have difficulty saying "no", examining what the word "yes" means is helpful as "yes" and "no" are part of the same continuum.

Some people have little or no difficulty with the word "no" while "yes" causes much internal conflict. This may be due to issues of:

1) promises, e.g., "When I say 'yes', I feel like it's a promise, and I found out a long time ago that I can't trust promises"; 2) commitments, e.g., "I can't commit to one person without possibly hurting another" or "I can't commit to one person without feeling I will lose my sense of self" and 3) unresolved anger, e.g., "I won't say 'yes' because I don't want them to have my support."

To assist you toward greater insight, complete the following sentences:

When I say "yes", I _____

_____

_____

When I say "yes", I _____

_____

_____

When I say "yes", I _____

_____

_____

## "Yeses"
### EXERCISE 55

Think about "yeses" you've heard in your young life, e.g. a "yes" to be able to go on a trip with friends, a "yes" to have a particular toy or a "yes" to go on dates.

List five examples of "yeses" from your childhood and adolescence that were inappropriate:

1. _____

_____

2. _____

_____

3. _____

_____

**REPEAT AFTER ME**

4. _____
   _____

5. _____
   _____

List five examples of "yeses" from your childhood that were inappropriate:

1. _____
   _____

2. _____
   _____

3. _____
   _____

4. _____
   _____

5. _____
   _____

Have "yeses" in your life caused you any problems? Explain:

_____
_____
_____
_____
_____
_____
_____
_____
_____
_____

Have "yeses" turned out to be helpful? Explain:

_____

_____

_____

_____

_____

_____

_____

_____

_____

How did your mother say "yes"? Did she say "yes" only by never saying a clear "no"? Did she always have to get an answer from your father? Did she say "yes" to everything?

Write about hearing "yes" from your mom.

_____

_____

_____

_____

_____

_____

_____

_____

_____

**REPEAT AFTER ME**

How did your father say "yes"? Did he always say "yes"? Did he tend to say "yes" but attach a warning? Was he fair?

Write about hearing "yes" from your dad.

_____

_____

_____

_____

_____

_____

_____

_____

_____

As an adult, what do you hear when people say "yes" to you?

How do you feel? Explain:

_____

_____

_____

_____

_____

_____

_____

_____

_____

_____

_____

_____

_____

_____

**PRACTICING "NO" AND "YES"**

Now that you have an understanding of what the words "no" and "yes" mean to you, you may discover that you'd like to be able to use either word more frequently and feel good about it. Practice saying your word, "No" or "Yes", in front of a mirror. Say it louder. Louder. Louder. For people not used to using the words, it's important to practice saying them in order that when needed, the appropriate word comes "sliding" out. Don't just practice it prior to knowing that you want to use it. Practice it now — so that you'll have the option to use it at any time.

View these words as a part of you, just as feelings are a part of you — they're to be your friend, not your foe.

## EXERCISE 56

If "No" is difficult for you to say, complete:

It is okay to say "No!" When I say "No", I will feel better about myself because _____

_____

_____

It is okay to say "No!" When I say "No", I will feel better about myself because _____

_____

_____

It is okay to say "No!" When I say "No", I will feel better about myself because _____

_____

_____

Only after you have completed writing what "no" has meant in your life, become comfortable with verbalizing the word, and believe in the value of the word "no", will you begin to apply the words "yes" and "no" appropriately.

List four situations in which you would like to say, "no", e.g., when you are asked to go to a restaurant you aren't fond of, when you are asked to work during your lunch time.

1. _____

_____

2. _____

_____

3. _____

_____

4. _____

_____

Prioritize these situations in order of difficulty, (#1 being the easiest to do, #4 being the most difficult for you to do). Do this on a weekly basis, and begin saying "no" to the less difficult situations.

## EXERCISE 57

If "Yes" is difficult for you to say, complete:

It is okay to say "Yes"! When I say "Yes", I will feel better about myself because _____

_____

_____

It is okay to say "Yes"! When I say "Yes", I will feel better about myself because _____

_____

_____

It is okay to say "Yes"! When I say "Yes", I will feel better about myself because _____

_____

_____

List four situations in which you would like to say "yes", e.g., when you are asked to go to a party or when asked to join a group.

1. _____

_____

2. _____

_____

3. _____

_____

4. _____

_____

Prioritize these situations in order of difficulty, (#1 being the easiest to do, #4 being the most difficult for you to do). Do this on a weekly basis, and begin saying "yes" to the less difficult situations.

## Inappropriate Behavior — Childhood
## EXERCISE 58

It is common for a child in a dysfunctional family to learn to accept other people's unhealthy behavior without questioning it. This is often referred to as the development of a "high tolerance for inappropriate behavior". These children are taught well — Don't think, Don't question.

Reflect on situations which took place for you as a child and/or adolescent at which time you did not see someone else's behavior as inappropriate, but in thinking about it now, it is obvious that it was inappropriate. List four examples:

1. _____
_____
_____
_____

2. _____
_____
_____
_____

3. _____
_____
_____
_____

4. _____
_____
_____
_____

## Inappropriate Behavior — Adulthood
### EXERCISE 59

It is common that if you developed a high tolerance for inappropriate behavior as a child that you will continue that pattern today.

List examples of situations you have experienced as an adult in which someone's behavior was inappropriate:

1. _____

   _____

   _____

2. _____

   _____

   _____

3. _____

   _____

   _____

4. _____

   _____

   _____

## Intrusive Behavior

### EXERCISE 60

While some people don't question others' behavior at all, some people haven't learned a healthy respect for other people's boundaries. It is difficult for intrusive people to self-identify intrusive behavior. Ask yourself these questions: "Do I intrude on other people? Am I inconsiderate, and therefore, rude?"

Some people blatantly intrude, e.g., invite themselves to spend the night, while others intrude in a more passive style, e.g., attempt to relieve another person of unpleasant feelings, before that person has had a chance to verbalize them. Under the guise of caring and wanting to help someone the helper could be intrusive, particularly if the motivation for caring is to be noticed or to receive approval.

To be able to recognize our own intrusive behavior, it is easier when we can first identify it in others:

Examples:
— When you wanted privacy in bathing, your mother insisted on being able to enter the bathroom at any time.
— A sister took your toys to her room without asking and didn't return them.
— Dad would walk in and change the television station even though the kids were engrossed in a show.

List examples of intrusive behavior that took place in your family:

1. _____

_____

_____

2. _____

_____

_____

3. _____

_____

_____

4. _____

_____

_____

As you are identifying more inappropriate behavior, you are learning to identify the "intruding" person.

## EXERCISE 61

Name three people with whom you, as an adult, find yourself often having to say "no" to or with whom you must set limits:

1. _____

2. _____

3. _____

One could rationalize that these three people have an amazing capacity to ask for what they need — yet it could be that they are highly intrusive. People can ask for what they need without being intrusive. No one likes hearing a "no" — but a healthy person can respect your needs. Intrusive people push for their needs, not recognizing and not caring about others.

If you are intrusive, you may not be aware of this behavior. You may have attitudes that incorporate communal ownership. "This is my house, and I can do what I want, when I want." "Being family, they won't mind." "They have a lot of time, so it will be O.K." Intrusive people make generalized assumptions that help to assure they get what they want.

If you identify with the previous attitudes and are questioning whether or not you are intrusive, you may need to seek the help of a close friend. Ask the friend to help you identify those instances when you were intrusive and made assumptions about their time or their belongings.

You will live in perpetual fear that other people will not respond to your needs unless you gain a respect for others and establish an appropriate set of limits for them and yourself.

**REPEAT AFTER ME**

You may have practiced intrusive behavior in your adulthood. List four examples of your intrusive experiences:

1. _____

_____

_____

2. _____

_____

_____

3. _____

_____

_____

4. _____

_____

_____

If you identify with a high tolerance for inappropriate behavior, have difficulty knowing what appropriate behavior is / or find yourself being intrusive to others, then the key to stopping this behavior is learning to question. When you are in an uncomfortable or tenacious situation, STOP. Ask the following questions: Is this behavior okay with me? Are they being respectful of my feelings? Am I being respectful of their feelings and time? Before you can answer these questions honestly, you'll have to be able to identify feelings and feel a sense of your own worth. You have been working on these issues, so you soon should be ready for this.

## EXERCISE 62

You may want to keep a daily journal identifying what you have tolerated that was inappropriate or if you need to work on the other side of that continuum — when you have behaved in a manner that might have been intrusive to others. After completing each daily entry, note the feeling experienced in relation to the situation. If there was no feeling, note the fear you would have felt if you had not been so tolerant (or intrusive). Then identify an alternative response. Examples:

| **Tolerated Inappropriate Behavior** | **Demonstrated Intrusive Behavior** |
|---|---|
| I did not stick up for myself when my lover called me a name. | I assumed that my sister would babysit for me. I didn't ask ahead of time, although I knew I needed a sitter three days ago. |
| **Feeling or attitude:** Hurt, humiliation, anger | **Feeling or attitude:** Presumption. "She owes it to me, she's my sister." |
| **Alternative Behavior:** I could have said, "I am not a dumb . . . (so-and-so)" . . . (then assert my position) | **Alternative Behavior:** Asking my sister if she was available at the time I became aware of my need. |
| or | or |
| I could have said, "It is difficult for me to understand your position when you call me names." | Never assume my sister is obligated to babysit for me, and always consider it a favor. When I ask her to babysit, I must understand that she has priorities of her own. |

Sample journal entry format:

| **Tolerated Inappropriate Behavior** | **Demonstrated Intrusive Behavior** |
|---|---|

MONDAY

1. _____      1. _____

_____      _____

_____      _____

**Feeling or attitude:**      **Feeling or attitude:**

_____      _____

_____      _____

**Alternative Behavior:**      **Alternative Behavior:**

_____      _____

_____      _____

_____      _____

Do this exercise repeatedly.

After completing this to the extent that you clearly identify such situations, identify the options available (words verbalized and/or behaviors expressed) that would be appropriate responses. Repeat this for several situations.

## APOLOGIES

Apologies in dysfunctional family systems are often riddled with conflict. It is common to hear parents apologize verbally but continue hurtful behavior, to have one parent apologize for the other parent or not have apologies made when they were deserved.

Apologies very often are black/white issues for adult children. This is true because adult children often are people who always apologize or never apologize.

## EXERCISE 63

Complete the following sentences:

When my dad apologized, _____

_____

_____

When my mom apologized, _____

_____

_____

When my brother apologized, _____

_____

_____

When my brother apologized, _____

_____

_____

When my sister apologized, _____

_____

_____

When my sister apologized, _____

_____

_____

When I apologized, _____

_____

_____

_____

_____

## EXERCISE 64

What did apologies mean in your family? Who apologized to whom? Were apologies sincere? Did anything positive come from apologies? Write about this:

_____

_____

_____

_____

_____

_____

_____

_____

_____

_____

_____

_____

_____

_____

_____

_____

_____

_____

_____

_____

_____

_____

_____

_____

## Perpetual Apologies
## EXERCISE 65

If you are the perpetual apologizer, (a person who always apologizes), reflect on the instances as both a young person and adult person and note apologies you made but, in fact, were inappropriate as you were not at fault.

After you've listed situations where you apologized to "fix it", go back to each time frame and note what you fear would have happened if you had not apologized. Examples:

| **I apologized for** | **My fear was if I didn't apologize** |
|---|---|
| The time my dad hit my brother. | No one else would help my brother feel better. |
| The time I told my husband that he was intimidating the kids by yelling at them all of the time. | My husband would quit talking altogether — I couldn't stand the quiet tension. |

|  | **Apologies Made** | **Fear** |
|---|---|---|
| Birth-5 | _____ | _____ |
|  | _____ | _____ |
|  | _____ | _____ |
| 6-12 | _____ | _____ |
|  | _____ | _____ |
|  | _____ | _____ |
| 12-18 | _____ | _____ |
|  | _____ | _____ |
|  | _____ | _____ |
| 18-24 | _____ | _____ |
|  | _____ | _____ |
|  | _____ | _____ |

25-34 _____ _____

_____ _____

_____ _____

35-44 _____ _____

_____ _____

_____ _____

45-54 _____ _____

_____ _____

_____ _____

55-64 _____ _____

_____ _____

_____ _____

65 + _____ _____

_____ _____

_____ _____

If apologies are problematic for you in your adult life because you apologize for things for which you are not responsible, your focus needs to be on 1) resolving guilts, which includes accepting your ability/inability to impact things; 2) accepting responsibility for your anger and 3) eliminating your fears of rejection.

## EXERCISE 66

To assist you in identifying inappropriate situations for which you apologize, finish the following statements:

I don't need to apologize for _____

_____

_____ .

I don't need to apologize for _____

_____

_____ .

I don't need to apologize for _____

_____

_____ .

I don't need to apologize for _____

_____

_____ .

## Difficulty Apologizing
### EXERCISE 67

This exercise is for the adult child who has difficulty apologizing. Using these time frames, reflect on things you did or said (not thoughts or feelings you had, but something you did) for which you owe someone an apology:

Birth-5 _____

_____

_____

_____

6-12 _____

_____

_____

_____

12-18 _____

_____

_____

_____

18-24 _____

_____

_____

_____

25-34 _____

_____

_____

_____

35-44 _____

_____

_____

_____

45-54 _____

_____

_____

_____

55-64 _____

_____

_____

_____

65 + _____

_____

_____

_____

## EXERCISE 68

After you are finished with the previous exercise, write out an apology for each instance where an apology would have been appropriate. (Do this even if that person is deceased). Make it simple.

1. _____

_____

_____

_____

**REPEAT AFTER ME**

2. _____

_____

_____

_____

3. _____

_____

_____

_____

4. _____

_____

_____

_____

5. _____

_____

_____

_____

6. _____

_____

_____

_____

7. _____

_____

_____

_____

8. _____

_____

_____

_____

Using the following form, name the people to whom you owe apologies. Mark with a check (✔) the ones that you could apologize to in person, on the phone and/or in a letter. Now, mark with an "X" the ones to whom you still would not apologize. Note if the person is now deceased. Make your apology to the people whose names you have checked, and note the date.

Regarding those "X"'s, ask yourself what the fear is that keeps you from apologizing to those people. Once the fear is identified, share this fear with someone and ask yourself if the fear is realistic. After you've completed this process, go back to your list, and see if you can convert any of the "X"'s to "✔"'s.

| (✔)<br>Name of Person or Deceased<br>(X) | Nature of Apology | Date Accomplished |
| --- | --- | --- |
|  |  |  |

## Apology Letter
## EXERCISE 69

Should you want to apologize to a now-deceased person, do so in the form of a letter. Remember, there is no need to apologize for thoughts or feelings, only behaviors.

Dear _____ ,

    I want to apologize for _____

_____

_____

    I want to apologize for _____

_____

_____

    I want to apologize for _____

_____

_____

    I want to apologize for _____

_____

_____

Now that you have written the first letter, it's very important that you write a second letter to yourself from the deceased person. In this letter, this person will tell you that he/she forgives you for each infraction or instance that you are apologizing for.

Dear _____ ,

    I forgive you for the time _____

_____

_____

    I forgive you for the time _____

_____

_____

    I forgive you for the time _____

_____

_____

I forgive you for the time _____

_____

_____

## BLACK AND WHITE

It is common for adult children to think in black/white — not perceiving options, believing that only one "right" and one "wrong" option exists.

Everything is black or write — there's no in-between. When an adult child chooses to trust someone, he often does this with an "all or nothing" approach — totally trusting, revealing all his vulnerabilities or being so distrustful that he reveals no information about himself. Adult children bounce from feeling "in control" to "out of control", from feeling "great" to feeling "despair", with no stops in-between. Adult children are often unfeeling or overcome with feelings. They often experience a sense of being very "needy" to believing "they have no needs".

This "black/white" or "all or nothing" way of viewing things causes most people a great deal of difficulty.

Think about how black and white thinking evolved for you. For example, "my mother was either very nice to us or she totally ignored us"; "my father was a very loving, giving person when he was sober — when he was drunk, he was very mean, very violent, or he simply was absent;" "I did very well in school or I got into a lot of trouble."

## EXERCISE 70

Much black and white thinking stems from childhood beliefs that, "If I do one thing 'wrong' in my life, I might as well not bother with doing anything 'right', or "I must do it this way (there are no alternatives) or something very bad will happen."

That "something bad" that might happen, may be:

— my dad won't love me;

— my mom won't love me;

— I'll cry;

— I'll get angry;

— friends will make fun of me; or

— others will know what is happening here.

— _____

— _____

— _____

— _____

Circle any of the above issues if they were fears for you, and add any other fears to the list.

Reflecting on your early years, consider what thoughts and fears you experienced that may have contributed to your black/white thinking.

As a child . . .

1. I _____

or (would happen) _____ .

2. I _____

or (would happen) _____ .

3. I _____

or (would happen) _____ .

4. I _____

or (would happen) _____ .

5. I _____

or (would happen) _____ .

It is important to view things as part of a process, not seeing things as black/white or right/wrong. Black/white thinking becomes very rigid and leads toward feeling "crazy" as one bounces from one extreme to the other. Examples of black/white thinking are: "If I don't get to the dinner party it will be a disaster." Alternative thought: "If I don't get to the dinner party, I will be disappointed— so will others. But the food will get put on the table, and people will eat." "If I don't finish this by today, I'll totally mess up tomorrow's schedule." Alternative thought: "If this doesn't get done today, I'll have to rear-range tomorrow morning's schedule. By the end of the week, everything on the schedule will have been addressed."

List situations where you have a tendency to view things as black/white, all or nothing.

1. _____

_____

_____

2. _____

_____

_____

3. _____

_____

_____

4. _____

_____

_____

Acting on black/white views typically means moving in leaps and bounds rather than taking steps. Modifying all-or-nothing behavior means developing the ability to arrive at a balance point.

For example, if trust is a black/white issue, a balance point would be that you can trust some people with some things, but not with others. If anger is all or nothing — a balance point between "being fine" and "rage" is "frustration". If your need for people is a black/white issue, a new message may be "I have needs, some that are more important to me now than others; some that incorporate other people, some that do not." Go back to your list of black/white issues and identify a balanced thinking that demonstrates greater flexibility.

On a daily basis, reflect back at the end of each day on any black/white attitudes or behaviors you experienced. Identify other alternative thoughts. While hindsight may not correct the past situation, the act of learning to identify rigid thoughts and developing alternative perceptions will help you to begin to see options as they arise. You will soon see yourself becoming much more flexible.

# CHAPTER 5
# SPECIAL TOPICS

## Religion
## EXERCISE 71

Whether or not you were raised with the influence of a particular religion or faith, the concept of God is one usually shared by all people.

What church or synagogue did you attend as a child? _____

_____

If you were involved in religion as a child, describe your involvement. Was it:

| | | |
|---|---|---|
| Fun? | YES | NO |
| Scary? | YES | NO |
| Boring? | YES | NO |
| Meaningful? | YES | NO |

How was God (your concept of) perceived?     LOVING     PUNISHING     INDIFFERENT

Other _____ Elaborate _____

_____

_____

_____

_____

_____

_____

_____

Did you attend a church or synagogue only because your parents dictated your involvement? YES NO

## Early Religious Influence
EXERCISE 72

As a child or teenager, were there any particular rituals or ceremonies that were of special value or significance for you? What were they? How were they special?

_____

_____

_____

_____

_____

_____

_____

_____

_____

_____

_____

_____

_____

_____

_____

_____

_____

_____

_____

## EXERCISE 73

Looking back at your early religious influence, what parts are positive that are still with you today?

_____

_____

_____

_____

_____

_____

_____

_____

_____

_____

Are there any negative influences still with you?

_____

_____

_____

_____

_____

_____

_____

_____

_____

_____

_____

## Religion Today
EXERCISE 74

If your involvement in your church or synagogue stopped, what made you stop?

_____

_____

_____

_____

_____

_____

_____

Describe your feelings about religion and God today.

_____

_____

_____

_____

_____

_____

_____

Would you like to go back to church?        YES        NO

Explain _____

_____

_____

_____

_____

_____

_____

If your parents were involved in a self-help group such as AA, Al-Anon or Families Anonymous, what do you think about the "Higher Power" concept?

_____

_____

_____

_____

_____

_____

_____

It is essential for adult children in recovery to learn to have faith in a process, in something outside of ourselves. Otherwise, we don't recover. For many people, that faith may be in a "Higher Power" or "God". Others aren't sure — while you may be agnostic or have little faith in anything outside of yourself, be open to "not always controlling" and try to develop faith in a process. Trust that in time, healing, self love and love of others will become a part of your life.

## HOLIDAYS

Holidays are often a time of anxiety and depression. A reason for this is that holidays are often times for families to be together. Family gatherings on holidays imply that everyone must have a good time! "Having a good time together" is very difficult to accomplish when people have survived in an environment of dishonesty, unexpressed feelings, grief and abuse.

For family members who are distant or fearful of each other, holidays are a time of even greater deceit. In families where masks are a general rule, there is even greater need for masks on days that are taken aside to give and receive from each other, to play together, to relax.

For many kids, three-day weekends such as July 4th, Labor Day or Memorial Day mean a 3-day drunk vs. a 2-day drunk.

Valentine's Day may represent another time Dad gets to forget Mom.

Easter may represent the family going to church once this year.

Christmas means waiting to see if Mom stays sober or gets drunk before the Christmas dinner. It may mean needing to give Dad a present after he has slapped you around all year.

Holidays can certainly be happy times too. But they aren't, as a rule of thumb, for people in dysfunctional families.

## EXERCISE 75

Using the following list, use words that summarize what these holidays mean to you. (Add words of your own, if you wish):

| | | | | |
|---|---|---|---|---|
| depression | giving | food | happiness | presents |
| receiving | drinking | excitement | fun | violence |
| drunkeness | loneliness | vacation | party | picnic |
| fear | guilt | sadness | boredom | games |

|  | **As a Child** | **As an Adult** |
|---|---|---|
| 1. New Year's | _____ | _____ |
|  | _____ | _____ |
|  | _____ | _____ |
| 2. Washington's Birthday | _____ | _____ |
|  | _____ | _____ |
|  | _____ | _____ |
| 3. Easter | _____ | _____ |
|  | _____ | _____ |
|  | _____ | _____ |
| 4. Memorial Day | _____ | _____ |
|  | _____ | _____ |
|  | _____ | _____ |
| 5. July 4th | _____ | _____ |
|  | _____ | _____ |
|  | _____ | _____ |
| 6. Labor Day | _____ | _____ |
|  | _____ | _____ |
|  | _____ | _____ |
| 7. Thanksgiving | _____ | _____ |
|  | _____ | _____ |
|  | _____ | _____ |

8.  Christmas

    _____        _____

    _____        _____

    _____        _____

9.  Other religious holiday(s)    (if applicable)

    a. _____    _____        _____

    _____        _____

    _____        _____

    b. _____    _____        _____

    _____        _____

    _____        _____

    c. _____    _____        _____

    _____        _____

    _____        _____

10. Other Holidays

    a. _____    _____        _____

    _____        _____

    _____        _____

    b. _____    _____        _____

    _____        _____

    _____        _____

## Christmas (Past)
EXERCISE 76

Christmas is often a difficult time for people. The following exercises will help you explore old issues around this holiday:

1. Christmas was a time of _____

_____

_____

_____

2. At Christmas time, my dad _____

_____

_____

_____

3. At Christmas time, my mother _____

_____

_____

_____

4. At Christmas time, I _____

_____

_____

_____

5. At Christmas time, my brother _____

_____

_____

_____

6. At Christmas time, my brother _____

_____

_____

_____

7. At Christmas time, my sister _____

_____

_____

_____

8. At Christmas time, my sister _____

_____

_____

_____

9. The best part of the holiday was _____

_____

_____

_____

_____

10. The worst part of the holiday was _____

_____

_____

_____

_____

## Christmas (Present)

EXERCISE 77

What is Christmas like for you now?

1. Christmas is a time of _____

_____

_____

_____

_____

2. At Christmas time, I (with present family, spouse, lover) _____

_____

_____

_____

_____

3. Christmas time with my children is a time _____

_____

_____

_____

_____

_____

_____

_____

_____

4. The best part of the holiday is _____

_____

_____

_____

_____

5. The worst part of the holiday is _____

_____

_____

_____

_____

If you are happy with your Christmases today, you may go on to the next exercise. Otherwise, complete the following:

I'd like Christmas to be a time when _____

_____

_____

_____

In order for that to happen, I would have to _____

_____

_____

_____

Am I willing to do the above?     _____ Yes     _____ No     _____ Partially

If "no", what is my fear? _____

_____

_____

_____

If "no", what do I need to work on in order to make it a "yes"? _____

_____

_____

_____

_____

## Birthdays

EXERCISE 78

Birthdays are a day for us to feel special. We may continue with our daily responsibilities, but we can still take time to acknowledge our specialness. Birthdays are also times with which we experience difficulty. As adults, in order for us to enjoy our birthdays, we must resolve conflicts and incidents that occurred during our childhood birthdays.

Think about your birthdays as a child. Did you look forward to your birthdays? What did you want to happen? Did you enjoy them? Why? Were you disappointed? Why?

With these thoughts in mind, write about your birthdays as a child:

_____

_____

_____

_____

_____

_____

_____

_____

_____

_____

_____

_____

_____

_____

## EXERCISE 79

Write about any two birthdays before your 20th birthday that were positive and for that reason stand out for you:

_____

_____

_____

_____

_____

_____

_____

_____

_____

_____

Now, write about any two birthdays before your 20th birthday that you remember with sadness, disappointment or anger:

_____

_____

_____

_____

_____

_____

_____

_____

_____

_____

## REPEAT AFTER ME

As an adult, describe your attitude regarding birthdays for the past ten years.

_____

_____

_____

_____

_____

_____

_____

_____

_____

_____

Do any one or two stand out as particularly fun, happy or special?

Which  ones? _____ , _____

Explain what made them special:

_____

_____

_____

_____

_____

_____

_____

_____

_____

_____

Do any two birthdays stand out as particularly unhappy? Which two?

_____ , _____

Explain what made them unhappy:

_____

_____

_____

_____

_____

_____

_____

_____

_____

_____

_____

## EXERCISE 80

Please check your attitude:                                    YES          NO

Birthdays are to be celebrated.                            _____    _____

Birthdays are just another day.                            _____    _____

Birthdays are for kids.                                    _____    _____

Birthdays are great, as long as they're not mine.          _____    _____

I hate my birthday.                                        _____    _____

I like my birthday.                                        _____    _____

I feel special on my birthday.                             _____    _____

I try to forget my birthday.                               _____    _____

Other thoughts: _____

_____

_____

Regarding your next birthday, list options that you could exercise to make that day a special one for you.

1. _____

_____

2. _____

_____

3. _____

_____

## Bedtime

## EXERCISE 81

Bedtime carries with it a variety of memories. Most children have a consistent bedtime that will often become later in the evening as they grow older. Children know their bedtime and get themselves to bed — often with only a slight prodding by their parents. A child often says "goodnight" to parents, and when the child is young, perhaps that "goodnight" is accompanied by a kiss.

But in dysfunctional families, bedtimes are stressful times. Children often have inappropriate bedtimes such as 8:00 for a 15-year-old, or 11:00 for a 7-year old. Children may not have any consistent structure for bedtime, and as a result, they don't get the appropriate amount of sleep. Children often go to bed crying, afraid, angry and very lonely. Some children take animals, food or imaginary friends to bed in order to comfort themselves. Some kids stay up at night in bed waiting for a parent to come home or listening to other family members fighting. Prayers may be a bedtime ritual for children who are seeking a source from their grief or anxiety.

What was bedtime like for you between the ages of:

Before age 6 _____

_____

_____

_____

_____

_____

_____

6-10 _____

_____

_____

_____

_____

_____

_____

11-14 _____

_____

_____

_____

_____

_____

_____

## REPEAT AFTER ME

15-18 _____

_____

_____

_____

_____

_____

_____

**DINNER**

Dinner time means a variety of things to a variety of people. Examples:
— A time when the family could get together to share the day's experiences with each other.
— A time when Mom often worried about where Dad was.
— A time of silent tension.
— A time of arguing.


## EXERCISE 82

Complete the sentence for yourself:

As a kid, dinner was a time _____

_____

As a kid, dinner was a time _____

_____

As a kid, dinner was a time _____

_____

Please circle the appropriate response.

| | | |
|---|---|---|
| Was dinner looked forward to? | YES | NO |
| Was it a time to socialize? | YES | NO |
| Was it usually a positive time? | YES | NO |
| Was there often arguing? | YES | NO |
| Did people "eat and run"? | YES | NO |
| Did people eat at different times? | YES | NO |
| Did people eat together? | YES | NO |
| Was the time of dinner fairly regular? | YES | NO |
| Was clean-up and the responsibility for dinner shared among the entire family? | YES | NO |

## Dinnertime Picture

EXERCISE 83

Draw a picture that typifies what dinner time was like at your house when you were a child.

Give thought to the location, who sat next to whom, what you typically had to eat, the topic of dinner conversation and who did the talking, the dinner time mood.

## EXERCISE 84

Complete the following:

As an adult, dinner is a time of _____

_____

As an adult, dinner is a time of _____

_____

As an adult, dinner is a time of _____

_____

Please circle the appropriate response:

| | | |
|---|---|---|
| As an adult, do I look forward to dinner? | YES | NO |
| Is it a time to socialize? | YES | NO |
| Is it usually a positive time? | YES | NO |
| Is there a lot of arguing? | YES | NO |
| Do people "eat and run" (present family)? | YES | NO |
| Do people eat at different times (present family)? | YES | NO |
| Do people eat together (present family)? | YES | NO |
| Is the time of dinner fairly regular? | YES | NO |
| Is the responsibility and clean-up for dinner shared among the entire family? | YES | NO |

## EXERCISE 85

In 3-5 sentences, describe a wonderful dinner:

_____

_____

_____

_____

_____

_____

_____

What will it take to have a dinner like that?

_____

_____

_____

_____

_____

_____

_____

_____

Give yourself a time frame to accomplish the above, then make that wonderful dinner a reality.

Dinner can be a nice time if you let it be.

## FOOD

While dinner was often riddled with tension, the act of eating, for many people, became symbolic. People raised in unhappy homes and people who are unhappy will often eat for emotional reasons rather than for physical need. Food can become a source of nurturing. In essence, may people stuff their feelings with food, and find emotional comfort and solace in eating. The act of eating may become self-destructive and encourage self-hatred. While most people who become self-destructive via food do this by overeating, some people attempt to compensate for their overeating by ''purging'' — vomiting, becoming what is known as ''bulimic''. Others demonstrate their self-destructiveness by a form of starvation which often results in anorexia. Everyone needs to reflect on what food means to them. Should food be a problem in your life, it is important that you seek help with specialists in this field (call local crisis line for eating disorder clinics).

## Eating Habits
EXERCISE 86

As a child and teenager, I ate: (Circle one)

| A great deal more than necessary | More than necessary | An appropriate amount | Less than normal | Was often hungry |
|---|---|---|---|---|

If you ate more or less than normal, write about that. Why do you think this occurred? What did eating (or not eating) do for you?

_____

_____

_____

_____

_____

_____

Is your pattern of eating the same or different today? _____

If the same, what does eating or not eating do for you today?

_____

_____

_____

_____

_____

If it is different, how has it changed?

_____

_____

_____

_____

_____

## EXERCISE 87

What was your parents' attitude about thin people?

Mom _____

Dad _____

What was your parents' attitude about fat people?

Mom _____

Dad _____

What messages did your parents give you about what to eat?

Mom _____

Dad _____

What messages did your parents give you about when to eat?

Mom _____

Dad _____

How do you feel about thin people?

_____

_____

_____

How do you feel about fat people?

_____

_____

_____

What messages do you give yourself about what to eat?

_____

_____

_____

_____

What messages do you give yourself about when to eat?

_____

_____

_____

_____

Be aware — if you consistently eat out of loneliness, anger, fear or to escape; if you eat to feel better — and that's all you know to do to feel better, you may need additional help to find ways of expressing feelings, liking yourself and getting your needs met.

## Money
## EXERCISE 88

How one values money — the acquiring and spending of it — is often related to how money was acquired and spent in your family.

The following questions will help you to explore possible connections of the past to the present:

How did your father earn money? _____

Did you have any strong feelings about how he earned money or the amount that he earned? _____

_____

How did your dad spend money? Did you have any strong feelings about this spending? _____

_____

_____

_____

Pertaining to both earning and spending:

I wished he would have _____

_____

_____

_____

I wished he wouldn't have _____

_____

_____

_____

## EXERCISE 89

How did your mom earn money? _____

_____

Did you have any strong feelings about how she earned money or the amount she earned? _____

_____

How did your mom spend money? Did you have any strong feelings about this spending? _____

_____

_____

_____

Pertaining to both earning and spending:

    I wished she would have _____

    _____

    _____

    _____

    I wished she wouldn't have _____

    _____

    _____

    _____

## EXERCISE 90

When did you first have any of your own money? How did you get it? What did you do with it? _____

_____

_____

_____

_____

_____

_____

_____

_____

_____

_____

Were you embarrassed and wished your family had more or less money?

_____

_____

_____

_____

If your family had more money, how would that have affected your family?

_____

_____

_____

_____

## Money Today

### EXERCISE 91

The following statements may help you assess your present attitudes regarding money:

T     F     I hate to spend money.

T     F     I make sure I always pay my own way.

T     F     I seldom spend money on myself.

T     F     I seldom spend money on anyone else.

T     F     I can never keep any money; I spend whatever I have.

T     F     I am afraid of not having enough money.

T     F     I am afraid of having more money than I really need.

T     F     I have no strong feelings about money — good or bad.

Describe your financial situation today.

_____

_____

_____

_____

_____

Do you have any financial fears? Explain:

_____

_____

_____

_____

_____

## EXERCISE 92

How similar or dissimilar are your financial issues to those of your parents? Explain.

_____

_____

_____

_____

_____

_____

_____

_____

_____

_____

## PETS

Pets are often very important to children. They usually become very significant in the lives of children whose needs aren't being met by people. A pet can be our friend who listens to all we have to say — without offering judgment. Pets love us unconditionally. Many times pets can be held, and sometimes they lick the tears from our faces. They are often warm and cuddly.

## EXERCISE 93

What animals did you have as you were growing up? Were they family pets or your pets specifically? List all of your pets and describe your relationship with them:

_____

_____

_____

_____

_____

_____

_____

_____

_____

_____

_____

_____

_____

_____

_____

## Safe Places

## EXERCISE 94

Sometimes we found a particular place at home to go for a sense of safety — a closet, under the bed, in a tree house, under the porch. Did you have any such place? Write about this place — where it was and the security you felt when you were there:

_____

_____

_____

_____

_____

_____

_____

_____

_____

_____

_____

## THOUGHTS ABOUT DEATH

When you live in a home where you are frightened a great deal, it is very common to think of death. Kids will often wish that a particular family member would die — believing life would then be better. Sometimes they believe life would be better for all concerned if they themselves died. Some kids even think about the way in which someone will die.

Children are often afraid of their own death or the death of other family members. They often have valid reasons for such fears if they see a parent drink and drive, pass out while holding lit cigarettes, fighting, attempting suicide or threatening physical abuse.

## EXERCISE 95

As a child, were you ever afraid that you would die?     YES     NO

Were you ever afraid that one of your parents would die?     YES     NO

If yes, which one? _____

Were you ever afraid that one of your brothers or sisters would die?     YES     NO

If yes, which one? _____

Write about these fears:

_____

_____

_____

_____

_____

_____

_____

_____

As a child, do you remember ever wishing that you would die?          YES          NO

Do you remember ever wishing that one of your parents would die?          YES          NO

If yes, which parent? _____

Do you remember ever wishing that one of your brothers or sisters would die?          YES          NO

If yes, which one? _____

Write about these thoughts. In doing so, remember this is common — and you obviously were very frightened and angry. That's OK.

_____

_____

_____

_____

_____

_____

_____

_____

_____

_____

_____

_____

_____

The reality of your own death is even more real if someone close to you dies.

A death in the family will severely disrupt a family. There is much loss — whether the death was anticipated or sudden, whether it was the death of a young child or a parent. Such a loss is one of the ultimate challenges of any family. The challenge comes in being able to grieve openly, restabilize and continue to reintegrate the now-present family. If the death occurs in a family which is affected by mental illness, physical/sexual abuse or alcoholism, the grief process is greatly stifled and seldom resolved. The problem of alcoholism, abuse, mental illness, etc., often worsens when a family death occurs. If you experienced the death of a loved one in an affected family when you were young, it is most likely that you would benefit by talking with a professional experienced in grief work.

## TOUCH

People will receive touch in a variety of ways. Positive touches are hugs, hand-holding, pats on the back, a rub of the head, lap sitting or sitting close to another.

Negative touches are slaps, pinches, kicks, slugs or being slammed against the wall.

Kisses can be negative or positive — kisses hello or goodnight may have pleasant memories. Yet some kisses and hugs may be associated with drunkeness, guilt or manipulation.

Children may experience sexual connotations with kisses, hugs and being touched. This is confusing, scary and guilt-inducing. Some children experience direct sexual experiences with other family members — experiences with fondling, oral sex or intercourse. This is incest.

Sometimes there is simply no touching in a family.

## EXERCISE 96

Please write about what touch represented to you as a child. Make reference to touch between you and your mother, father, siblings and any other significant family member:

Mother: _____

_____

_____

_____

_____

_____

_____

Father: _____

_____

_____

_____

_____

_____

_____

Brothers (name individual brothers): _____

_____

_____

_____

_____

_____

_____

Sisters (name individual sisters): _____

_____

_____

_____

_____

_____

_____

Extended family members (name family members): _____

_____

_____

_____

_____

_____

_____

## Picture of Touch

EXERCISE 97

Do a collage or draw a picture about what being touched represented to you as a child.

Examples:
1) a picture of a woman hugging a child may represent that your mother hugged you a lot.
2) a picture of a school graduation may indicate you were only hugged at ceremonial events.
3) a picture of a large hand may represent that you were slapped with an open hand
4) a picture of a teddy bear may represent that you were seldom touched and you used a stuffed animal for physical nurturing.

## Touching People
## EXERCISE 98

This exercise is designed in order for you to give thought to how you may touch the people in your life. Using the following words, note the style you tend to use with people, male and female, recognizing that touch will vary with individual people:

**WORDS:**

| | | |
|---|---|---|
| Kiss | Handshake | Slap |
| Hug | Don't Touch | Hit |
| Pat (on arm, leg shoulder, etc.) | Pinch | Kick |
| | Sexual | |

| PEOPLE | MALE | FEMALE |
|---|---|---|
| Acquaintances | _____ | _____ |
| Friends | _____ | _____ |
| Professional Associates | _____ | _____ |
| Parents | _____ | _____ |
| Brother/Sister (name) | | |
| _____ | _____ | _____ |
| _____ | _____ | _____ |
| _____ | _____ | _____ |
| _____ | _____ | _____ |
| Extended Family Members | _____ | _____ |
| | _____ | _____ |
| Spouse/Lover | _____ | _____ |
| Your children (name individually) | | |
| _____ | _____ | _____ |
| _____ | _____ | _____ |
| _____ | _____ | _____ |
| _____ | _____ | _____ |

## EXERCISE 99

Are you comfortable with touching people? Would you like your touching to be different, and with whom? Elaborate:

_____

_____

_____

_____

_____

_____

_____

_____

_____

_____

_____

_____

_____

_____

_____

_____

_____

_____

_____

_____

_____

_____

_____

## INCEST

Incest is both frightening and traumatic for the victim. If you were an incest victim, and you never have talked about this to anyone or have only begun to broach the subject of incest on a superficial level, it is highly recommended that you call the local crisis line and ask about services and support groups for people who were victims of incest as children. Incest victims need to be involved in a therapeutic process and be part of an on-going support system. Incest, even if it occurred once, is usually very traumatizing and often will have long-range consequences. It's important that you have the opportunity to talk about what happened.

Incest occurs in many families and is even more likely to occur in alcoholic families.* Incest is typically male-to-female, though it can be female-to-male, male-to-male and female-to-female. It is usually father/stepfather-to-daughter, though it can be mother-to-child, extended family member (grandparent/uncle-to-child) and it can be sibling-to-sibling. Sometimes a child is being offended by more than one person. It often lasts several years.

If you were an incest victim, it is important for you to recognize that:

1) You were a child, with only the emotional, mental and physical defenses of a child.

2) You are not at fault!

Some children were sexually molested by non-family members. Many times, this begins in a friendly way that becomes confusing, humiliating and frightening. Again, whatever the ploy used to manipulate you, e.g., "you are my friend, let's play", "I like you, don't you like me?" or by force, these "friends" are in the wrong and they are responsible.

It is vital that incest and molestation issues be addressed with the aid of a support group and a helping professional.

## BATTERING

If you were raised in a home where people were hit, slapped, punched or pushed, it is very common to find that same pattern repeated in your own adult life.* You did not have to be the person hit to have been affected — you may have been the nondirect victim by witnessing the abuse. When battering repeats itself, you may become the offender, the direct victim (being abused) or the indirect victim (witnessing another family member being hit).

If battering is happening in your adult life or you live in fear of it being repeated, it is vital that you seek professional help. You deserve freedom from such fear and abuse.

*This subject is covered in greater detail in Chapter 7 of *It Will Never Happen to Me.*

## DRINKING

Becoming dependent on alcohol and other drugs is an insidious process. Many people are able to use alcohol and other drugs and not become dependent. Nonetheless, a very large number of people will become chemically dependent. Total abstinence from alcohol and drugs is the only defense against dependency. However, since most people will use alcohol or drugs, they develop a perspective that they'll have the self control and willpower not to abuse or become dependent. All of the best intentions, self control and intelligence won't keep people from chemical dependency. While it can happen to anyone, dependency is most prevalent in families where there is parental or grandparental alcoholism.

While this is more fully addressed in *It Will Never Happen To Me,* the causes for alcohol and drug dependency seem to be found in a combination of genetic and environmental factors.

The following are three questions that are often asked:

— Do you drink to have fun?
— Do you drink to relax?
— Do you drink to escape?

These are not uncommon reasons for drinking, but additional clues to the possibility that drinking or using may become a problem may be found in the following questions:

— Do you find ways to have fun that don't include drinking?

(Some people may say, "Sure, I bowl". But is it common that the bowling is rewarded after-wards by getting drunk?)

— Do you find ways to relax that don't include drinking or using?

(Some people say that they watch TV to relax and forget to mention that they light up a joint several times in the process.)

— Do you find other avenues to escape that don't include drinking?

(Again, this requires total honesty.)

If you answer "no" to any of the above questions, the author suggests you take this signal seriously and begin to find alternative forms of fun, relaxation or escape. Should you answer "no" to two or three of the questions, it is suggested you seek help to explore your use of alcohol and other drugs.

## GENERATIONAL ASPECT

Children who develop a high sense of tolerance for inappropriate behavior often, as adults, have great difficulty recognizing problems until they reach crisis proportions. These people repeatedly give another person or situation the "benefit of the doubt" before they hear their own inner cries of danger.

Typically, alcoholics and drug abusers practice their dependency for years before the alcoholism or drug addiction is identified as a problem. Often physical and/or sexual abuse exists within a family for a long time before it is seen as more than a "one-time-only incident that won't be repeated again". Anorexia and bulimia can be hidden for years and often aren't identified until late-stage physical problems manifest themselves. Overeaters consistently demonstrate the most visible symptom of an eating disorder yet, they too, can live with obesity for several years before they believe that they are in a crisis.

Should you even suspect that you have symptoms of a problem that is generational in your family — should you get any feedback from other people that suggests the possibility of this problem — be open to asking for help so that you are not alone in resolving the problem.

# CONCLUSION

It is most likely that weeks and probably months have passed since you first picked up *REPEAT AFTER ME* and began your process of reflection. Many readers will find it helpful to do some of the exercises a second or third time over the next year or two. Recovery is an ongoing process and takes time. Be patient with yourself. Be willing to recognize your strengths. Find support systems to validate your feelings and perceptions. Begin to risk more of yourself. Try new behaviors that will allow your needs to be met.

As mentioned in the introduction, we must acknowledge our past — our childhood — grieve the losses and take responsibility for how we live our lives today. Today, you and the child within you deserve . . .

to play . . .

to laugh . . .

to relax . . .

to be flexible . . .

to develop the ability to
lead yet feel comfortable
when it is time to follow . . .

to question . . .

to talk honestly . . .

to make decisions . . .

to attend to your own needs . . .

to understand where your power
lies . . .

to protect yourself . . .

to know and accept your feelings
and to be able to express those
feelings . . .

to no longer live your life in fear and

to believe in your specialness . . .